Fulfil Me Fully, Phil
Playing With…
$ellebrity

Three plays by Sebastian Rex

Published by Playdead Press 2012

A CIP catalogue record for this book is available from the British Library.

ISBN 978-0-9574491-3-8

Playdead Press
www.playdeadpress.com

Contents

Foreword

In his four previous works to *Fulfil Me Fully, Phil*, Sebastian Rex addresses extreme areas of modern urban life where in various ways those who are powerful exert themselves to hurt those who are weak. The qualities that make these plays remarkable are the value of his ideas, his alert command of language, plot and stagecraft, and a readiness to spring unnervingly comic developments into his plots.

In *Living With…*, the first of the four plays I have seen and admired, the Everyman figure is passively enduring humiliation from his flat mates. One of these starts cramming fistfuls of cake into his ever-open mouth, and this extraordinary incident is both appalling and astonishingly funny.

The focus in *Toy Boy* is on another passive male, dutifully accepting his role as sexual object, and one of the uncommon qualities in this play is that the hero's bid for freedom is marked by his shift from speaking in rhymed couplets to prose. The play confirmed Sebastian as a writer with a distinct and intriguing vision.

The sole male in *$ellebrity* is passive against his will, tied up by two women determined to have sex with him. The development here was more straightforward although, as with all his work, one could never be sure that events might not take a seriously alarming turn.

In *Spare* – the title an anagram of 'rapes' – he develops his analysis of bad relationships in an unprecedented manner. Parents exploit children, doctors their patients, friends prove treacherous and cruel, but the parts are all written gender-neutral and as a result Parent could be played by a male actor, in which case he will be a father; a female actor will make her a mother. This expresses Sebastian's argument that exploitation, ridicule and contempt is directed by bullies of either sex upon victims of either sex and abuse is to be found anywhere and everywhere. The play is printed in a separate volume with his adaptation of the Büchner classic – *The Woyzeck*

The richness of his ideas, intensity of vision and the precision of his direction confirm what I felt when I first came upon his plays, that here is a playwright with important messages to convey and with the skill and imagination to do this so vividly that the images he creates stay long in the mind.

Jeremy Kingston, critic for *The Times*

Fulfil Me Fully, Phil

Fulfil Me Fully, Phil was first performed at the Space, London 27th November 2012. The cast was as follows:

Cast

FATSO	Matt Lord
CHAIRMAN KESH	Ed Sheridan
BAKER	Kate Sandison
FIRST WHORE	Julie Ross
SECOND WHORE	Eamon Ali
HUSBAND	Steve Jesson
DOCTOR HIIL	Avita Jay
CAPTAIN KYIL	Joshua Ross Grocott
SISTER FATHER	Clare Harlow
THE SUICIDER	Milo Burridge
WIFE	Julia Stone
PHIL	Rhys Lawton

Creative Team

Writer/Director	Sebastian Rex
Assistant Director	Saskia Marland
Set Designer	Anna Soboleva
Costume Designer	Faye Bradley
Composer	Noam Galperin
Lighting Designer	Nic Farman
Casting Assistant	Rhona Foulis

Cast

Eamon Ali - Second Whore:

Eamon's recent theatre credits include: *66 Minutes in Damascus* (Shoreditch Town Hall/LIFT); *Titus Andronicus* (Etcetera Theatre); 'Sebastian' in *Twelfth Night* (Cockpit Theatre); *Time Warner Ignite 5 – Body Corporate* (Waterloo East Theatre); *The 24 Hour Plays: Old Vic New Voices* (Old Vic); 'Arthur' in *Kid Arthur & the Knights of the Revolution* (The Space); 'Alex' in *A Clockwork Orange* (Southwark Playhouse). Recent film includes: *Hashtag Riot* (Toaster Productions); *Pini* (Pini Productions); *No Snow This Year* (LFS).

Milo Burridge - The Suicider:

Milo did the Foundation Course at RADA and a course at the Lee Strasberg Theatre and Film Institute in New New York, after being a member of the National Youth Theatre for several years. This is his professional theatrical debut.

Clare Harlow - Sister Father:

Clare trained at Mountview. Theatre credits include: *Gormenghast* (Blackshaw); *Thomas Hardy, Three Tales* (Blue Hills Theatre); *Daughters of Albion* (Wilton's Music Hall); 'Abigail' in *The Crucible* (Norwich Playhouse/tour); 'Jane' in *Jane Eyre* and *A Christmas Carol* (Brockley Jack); *The Deep Blue Sea* (Vaudeville Theatre, West End/tour); *Little Women* and *The Railway Children* (National No.1 tours for Theatreworks); *Love's Labour's Lost* (tour); *Babe, the Sheep-pig* (Rose Theatre, Kingston/tour). Film includes: *Lament* (Story Ark Productions); *The Judge* (Faith Drama).

Avita Jay - Doctor Hill:

Avita trained at Drama Studio London. Theatre credits include: *Spare* (New Diorama Theatre); Bardathon (The Scoop); *Toad* (Southwark Playhouse); *Sunday Morning at the Centre of the World* (Southwark Playhouse, Battersea Arts Centre, Tara Arts); 'Mistress Ford' and 'Anne Page' in *The Merry Wives of Windsor* (National Tour); Londonee (Rich Mix); Three Women (Etcetera Theatre). Film/TV credits include: L8R (BBC2 Learning Zone); *London, Paris, New York* (Fox Star Studios); *Twenty8K* (Formosa Films). She also records audiobooks for the RNIB.

Steve Jesson - Husband:

Steve trained at The Bridge Theatre Training Company in London. Credits while studying include: 'Malcolm' in *Macbeth*; 'Starveling' in *A Midsummer Night's Dream*; 'Duncan'/'David' in *Love And Money*. Since graduating he has appeared at the Camden Fringe; an art installation (Geneva Contemporary Arts Centre); *....Dream* (St. Leonards Church, Shoreditch); 'Folial' in *Escurial/School For Buffoons* (Lord Stanley); 'Mr. Stevens' in *The Devil Inside Him* (White Bear); short films and BBC/Channel 4 dramas.

Rhys Lawton - Phil:

Rhys has appeared on stage, film and in viral internet films with BBC Comedy and MSN. He was recently part of a three month weekly rep project with Charles Vance Productions, most notably playing 'Garry Essendine' in *Present Laughter* and 'Leonard' in *Time and Time Again*. He is currently working on *Underlondon*, a surreal puppet show and *Three Plays That Are Definitely Not About Snakes*.

Matt Lord - Fatso:

Matt has recently finished *The Regent's Canal* (a folk opera) and *Just Beneath Dogs* for London Irish Theatre, and has taken part in several short films. Other theatre credits include 'Mr. Lenville/Charles Cheeryble' in *Nicholas Nickleby* and 'Cleante' in *Tartuffe* (The Space); 'Hastings' in *Cromwell's Tour of Ireland*; 'Surgeon/Liver in The Body' (Henley on Thames Festival); 'Old Shepherd' in *The Winter's Tale* (Love Brixton Theatre Company).

Julie Ross – First Whore:

Julie trained at The Independent Theatre, Sydney. Theatre credits include *Evita* and *Jesus Christ Superstar* (Australasian tours); 'Bloody Mary' in *South Pacific* (Aberystwyth); 'Buttercup Grogan' in *The Unsinkable Molly Brown* (Landor); 'Matron' in *Be My Baby* (Colour House); 'Joanne' in *Company* and 'Phyllis' in *Follies* (Rose & Crown) and 'Angela' in *My Big Gay Italian Wedding* (Above the Stag). Julie also has a one-woman show *Don't Ask the Lady…!* Television credits include *Young Doctors* and *Sons and Daughters*.

Joshua Ross Grocott - Captain Kyil:

Joshua has been performing in youth and student theatre for the past fifteen years. Most recently he appeared in a play of his own creation, entitled *Pandemonium*, while studying at the University of Essex. Joshua has just completed his Creative Writing MA.

Kate Sandison - Baker:

Kate's West End credits include *Daisy Pulls it Off* (Arts Theatre); *Recipe for a Perfect Wife* (Charing Cross Theatre). Other theatre credits include *Lord Arthur Savile's Crime* (Barons Court); *Queen for a Day* (Upstairs at the

Gatehouse); *The Weir* (Southend Palace Theatre) and *An Ideal Husband* (Greenwich Playhouse). Feature Films include *The Cave* and *Death of the Virgin.* Shorts include the Bafta nominated *Speed Date.* She is an associate member of Nadine's Window Theatre Company.

Ed Sheridan - Chairman Kesh:
Ed trained at Drama Centre London and at the Anna Scher Theatre School prior to this, as well as spending time at the Vakhtangov Theatre in Moscow. He won the Judges' Award for Acting at last year's National Student Drama Festival, and also trained as a pianist at the Guildhall School of Music & Drama. He studied Classics at the University of Edinburgh.

Julia Stone - Wife:
Julia trained at Drama Studio London and has since performed in various theatre, television and short film productions. Theatre credits include *The Love Suicides at Sonezaki* (Wilton's Music Hall); *The Boy Friend* (Bridewell Theatre and tour); *Still I See My Baby* (Young Vic-Freshworks); *Farewell Sister* (New Diorama Theatre); The Nutcracker (Pentameters Theatre); Pygmalion (Middlesbrough Theatre and tour); and a rehearsed reading of *Passion* (King's Place).

Creative Team

Ina Berggren - Stage Manager:
Ina is a freelance Stage Manager who started her career in Sweden in 2005 but has been working in London since 2008. She has worked with Sebastian Rex for Acting Like Mad on *Spare and The Woyzeck* (New Diorama theatre); *Mind The Gap/Clichéd* (Blue Elephant Theatre). She has recently worked with Lazarus Theatre Company; Let Slip and Theatre Temoin and stage managed two shows at the 2012 Edinburgh Fringe Festival, *Machines For Living* and *The Fantasist.*

Faye Bradley - Costume Design:
Faye graduated from Bristol Old Vic Theatre School with an MA in Theatre Design. She recently designed the set and costumes for *4.48 Psychosis* (Drayton Theatre). Faye went to the Edinburgh festival to design *Silent Prayer of Poetry*. She designed the set for *The Good Soul of Szechuan* (Bristol old Vic Studio); the set and costumes for *The Yalta Game* (Alma Tavern Theatre) and the costumes for *Time and The Conways* (Circomedia).

Nic Farman - Lighting Design:
Nic is a recent graduate of the Rose Bruford College Lighting Design course. He has worked on a variety of different projects, ranging from new writing and classic play texts, to musicals, installations, promenade performance and movement-based pieces. His recent credits include: *Twelfth Night* (The Courtyard); *A Life in Monochrome* (the Space); *Laramie Project* (Leicester Curve) and *Casanova* (Lamorbey House).

Noam Galperin - Composer:
Noam trained at "The School For Jazz And Contemporary Music" in Israel, specializing in Composition and Arranging. He has been composing and arranging for theatre for the past 10 years. He has composed scores for various plays and several musicals. Noam has also Musically Directed, as well as orchestrated for several Musical Theatre Revues, and large tribute shows. Aside from theatre, Noam works with vocal ensembles, gospel choirs and solo singers. He has an album out, and two more on the way.

Saskia Marland - Assistant Director:
Saskia has recently graduated from Goldsmiths University with a first class degree in Drama and Theatre Arts. She comes from a dance and physical theatre background, and is passionate about the creation of new theatre, both as a performer and director. Other recent assisting credits include *Summer and Smoke* (Southwark Playhouse)

Mari Rettedal-Westlake - Creative Producer:
Mari graduated from Central School of Speech and Drama with an MA as a Creative Producer in 2006. She co-founded Space Productions in 2007 with Adam Hemming and has been the Creative Producer for most of their 15 productions to date including the successful transfer of *A Doll's House* to the Arcola in 2010. Mari also founded MADDID – a Nordic theatre company based in London. She is currently working as the Centre Manager at the Space.

Sebastian Rex - Writer/Director:
Sebastian Rex is a writer/director/choreographer as well as being the artistic director of Acting Like Mad and Sebastian Rex Dance Group. He also works as the Literary

Manager at The Space. In 2010 he was shortlisted for the Best Director Award at the Offies (Offwestend.com Theatre Awards) and in 2012 nominated for the Best Choreographer Award. He is also a recipient of a Peggy Ramsay foundation grant. **Writing/Directing credits include:** *The Woyzeck* and *Spare* (New Diorama Theatre); **Writing credits include:** *Mind The Gap* (Blue Elephant Theatre); **Directing credits include:** *Company* (Ye Olde Rose & Crown); *Kandicraft Jigsaw* (The Space). **Choreographing credits include:** *God Cried Woof; Clichéd; Modern Romance; I Wonder...* (Blue Elephant Theatre); *Just Don't; The Divine Comedy* (Robin Howard Theatre); *Love's Labour's Lost* (Tour).

Anna Soboleva - Set Design:
Anna was born and grew up in Riga, Latvia. She has a BA in Theatre Design from Nottingham Trent University and has worked with such companies as Archauz (Denmark); Lakeside Arts Centre (Nottingham); Grosman (Latvia) and Blind Summit (London). She recently designed *The Tempest* (The White Bear) and *The Woyzeck* (New Diorama Theatre). At the moment she is working on a project inspired by the life of Spanish Cubist Painter, Maria Blanchard.

The Space

The Space is a unique performance venue located on the Isle of Dogs providing for the diverse communities of Tower Hamlets and attracting audiences from all over London.

Our work as a venue centres on creating opportunities for new performers to present their work and staging exciting new versions of well-known stories through Space Productions. Our community outreach focuses on the development of theatre related skills through education and creating access for socially excluded or otherwise disadvantaged groups.

Space Productions is dedicated to staging accessible, ambitious and inventive theatre. To date the company has staged eleven productions of classic plays and well-known stories, providing a vital launchpad for emerging practitioners.

"The Space is a very exciting performing arts centre. Its attraction and dedication to the community is clear... this is a piece of theatre that is full of character and intrigue and succeeds in arousing opinions and beliefs in its audience. A promising and engaging production for an innovative space that certainly has some bright years ahead." Curtain Up

The Space Arts Centre
269 Westferry Road
London
E14 3RS
info@space.org.uk

The writer and Space Productions would like to thank;

Adam and all the volunteers and staff at the Space and Hubbub café
Jonathan Maimon, Alexander Mueller, Jeremy Kingston, Shapira-Reises, Gilat Vet, Niamh de Valera
David Byrne and all at New Diorama Theatre, Cornelia Baumann, Emma-Rachel Blackman, Tom Bonnington, Jennifer Burraston, Sarah Hall, David Hart, Adam Lilley, William Seaward, Rob Tucker
The Bush Theatre
Elliot Robinson and PlayDead Press

The writer would like to dedicate this publication to all the beautiful ones

Characters

Phil
Baker
Captain Kyil
Chairman Kesh
Fatso
Husband
Doctor Hiil
First Whore
Second Whore
Sister Father
The Suicider
Wife

ACT ONE
Scene 1 – Town Centre

We are in the town centre, which includes a bakery, a house and most noticeably, a door with a big sign saying 'Phil'

'Opening Song'

FATSO. *Good morning boys and girls*

CHAIRMAN KESH. *This is our town's centre*

BAKER. *This place is quite delightful*

FIRST WHORE. *Come on*

SECOND WHORE. *Let's go*

HUSBAND. *Do enter!*

DOCTOR HIIL. *We all live here in bliss*

CHAIRMAN KESH. *We live a perfect life*

SECOND WHORE. *We're happy all the time*

HUSBAND. *Except for me, I have no wife*

DOCTOR HIIL. *My name is Doctor Hiil*
I'm here if you feel ill

CAPTAIN KYIL. *And I am Captain Kyil*
Protecting you in the name of Phil

SISTER FATHER. *If you are in a crisis*
And need a comforting ear

BAKER. *This is Sister Father*
She's really quite a dear

FIRST WHORE. *If anyone is hungry*
The bakery's over there

FATSO. *But the cakes are too delicious*
So you better all beware

ALL. *We live a perfect life*
We're happy as can be
So please enjoy our town

SISTER FATHER. *And come to visit me*

CAPTAIN KYIL. *And me*

DOCTOR HIIL. *And me*

FATSO. *And me*

BAKER. *And me*

CHAIRMAN KESH. *And me*

HUSBAND. *And me*

FIRST WHORE. *And me*

SECOND WHORE. *And me*

FIRST WHORE. *No, me*

CAPTAIN KYIL. *I'm the happiest person*

SECOND WHORE. *I'm happier than him*

CHAIRMAN KESH. *I'm happier than both of them together*

THE SUICIDER. *(walks on and crosses out) I'm actually quite grim (exits)*

ALL. *We're always all so happy*
And that's all thanks to Phil
We've been happy since creation
And we're happy ever still
We're happy happy happy
Happy happy happy happy
Happy happy happy happy
Happy happ...

A long scream and a crash on the floor as THE SUICIDER falls off a tall building
THE SUICIDER lays motionless centre-stage
Standing around the body are HUSBAND, FATSO, CAPTAIN KYIL, BAKER and CHAIRMAN KESH
SISTER FATHER sits praying next to the door marked 'Phil'
TWO WHORES are standing leaning on the wall, uninterested in the events

BAKER. What a horrible way to end a life.

CAPTAIN KYIL. What a poor soul, having to jump off the building.

CHAIRMAN KESH. It must be at least twenty-storey-tall.

FATSO. Twenty-five.

BAKER. Twenty-five. What a horrible way to end a life.

HUSBAND. It's quite a shame that one tries to die. It really makes me wonder why.

FATSO. Un-happiness?

HUSBAND. Yes, I suppose that is the case for wanting to leave this worldly place.

DOCTOR HIIL runs in

DOCTOR HIIL. I came as soon as I heard. How is the patient?

CHAIRMAN KESH. Well, we think the patient is dead, Doctor Hiil.

DOCTOR HIIL. Has Sister Father given the verdict yet?

FATSO. No. Sister Father is still praying to Phil.

DOCTOR HIIL. So we can't know, can we!

CHAIRMAN KESH. The Suicider almost hit me. I could have died.

DOCTOR HIIL. Did any of you see what happened?

FATSO. I think the whores saw it.

DOCTOR HIIL. Oh… whores, did you see what happened?

FIRST WHORE. Piss off!

Long stop

CAPTAIN KYIL. It's a beautiful day.

BAKER. Oh, yes. Beautiful.

CHAIRMAN KESH. It would be a lovely day for a funeral.

FATSO. I love a good funeral…

SISTER FATHER finishes praying and joins the group

DOCTOR HIIL. Oh, Sister Father. What's the verdict?

SISTER FATHER. Not dead.

THE SUICIDER regains consciousness
BAKER, FATSO, CAPTAIN KYIL and HUSBAND exit disappointed

BAKER. What a waste of an afternoon. Now I must get back and reopen the bakery. And I was hoping to get an afternoon off.

CAPTAIN KYIL. Never mind, Baker, perhaps someone will die tomorrow instead.

FATSO. And Baker, take delight in knowing that I will enjoy your open bakery very much.

They exit

SISTER FATHER. It's a miracle! Thank Phil.

THE SUICIDER. A miracle?

CHAIRMAN KESH. You survived.

DOCTOR HIIL. You fell off a building. Twenty-five-storey-tall.

THE SUICIDER. Who survives falling off twenty-five-storey-tall buildings? This is a joke. A mad twist of fate's cruel knife.

SISTER FATHER. Or… a miracle!

THE SUICIDER. Sister Father, My survival is not a miracle. All it means is that I need to do a better job of my suicide.

SISTER FATHER. You don't see your survival as a miracle?

THE SUICIDER. I see it as a curse. A challenge. But fear not, I will not rest until I succeed. I have to work hard. I must think of cunning ways in which to kill myself. My suicide must be well crafted. It must be spectacular and genius. Thank you for setting me this challenge. Finally there's some meaning in my life. A point!

THE SUICIDER gets up and walks out

DOCTOR HIIL. I don't understand.

SISTER FATHER. Oh, Doctor Hiil, I'm not sure that went to plan.

DOCTOR HIIL. No, Sister Father. Not at all.

SISTER FATHER and DOCTOR HIIL exit

CHAIRMAN KESH. I could have died. What am I doing with myself? There are twenty-four hours in a day. I sleep for eight of them, travel for four, eat for one, take care of my body for one, work for ten, that leaves... oh dear. That leaves nothing for joy. But if I keep on working so much and doing all those things, I could go on holiday. Right. Let's start again. There are three hundred and sixty five days in a year. I work for two hundred and sixty days, I visit my family for ten, I worship Phil for sixty-eight, I am sick for fifteen, exhausted for seven, two are for thinking, and one for regrets. That leaves two days of holiday. Two days of joy. How wonderful. Two whole days in a year to live towards. Hold on. Two days out of three hundred and sixty five is less than one percent. That doesn't make any sense. I am wasting my time! I'm like the mule of the universe, wandering around and wondering why I'm not getting anywhere. My parents would be so disappointed in me if they saw me living on the farm of the universe eating universe hay. I can imagine my mother looking at me with sadness and my father with disgust, both saying, "Chairman, you are such a failure. Such a failure indeed." I am not a mule! I must make a success of myself. I must make enough money to move out of the farm and into the penthouse of the universe, where I could look at everybody from above and laugh. Ha! That's right. Ha!

Starts shouting

Buy something! Buy something!

THE SUICIDER passes by

Excuse me. Would you like to buy something?

THE SUICIDER. And what would I do with something? I'm going to be dead soon.

THE SUICIDER exits

CHAIRMAN KESH. Selling appears not to be as simple or as straightforward as I had first anticipated.

HUSBAND enters

CHAIRMAN KESH. Buy something from me.

HUSBAND. Shopping might help my depression. What do you have in your possession?

CHAIRMAN KESH. What would you like?

HUSBAND. I think your shirt is rather nice. Tell me, what would be its price?

CHAIRMAN KESH. How much do you think is fair for this beautiful shirt?

HUSBAND. I'll give you twenty notes for it. I do though hope that it will fit.

CHAIRMAN KESH. Oh, that is so much. I am joyful.

CHAIRMAN KESH takes off the shirt and gives it to HUSBAND in exchange for twenty notes and exits
HUSBAND stands lonely on stage

HUSBAND. I am alone, a lonely man. Trying to be happy, but I don't think I can. I so want to be in love, but I haven't received it from above. What is the point of living if you can't share your feeling? Aloneness and misery result in rhyming couplets and poetry. Why do these thoughts of loneliness bring out an immense sense of horniness? I want my horizons to expand, and I wouldn't mind having a different hand. What's the point of filling my existence if I can't share those feelings with some assistance? Oh, cruel world, please let me love. I pine for a wife, my own little dove. I demand you give some meaning to my life. Oh, cruel world, give me a wife!

WIFE enters

WIFE. Are you to be my husband?

HUSBAND. Are you to be my wife?

WIFE. I am.

HUSBAND. I am... happy. Not-so-cruel-world-after-all, thank you for turning my sadness into happiness in an instant. The introduction of a wife is all I needed to change my lyricism into prose.

As HUSBAND and WIFE exit to their home, HUSBAND shouts to the WHORES

Whores, look. I am happy!

SECOND WHORE. Piss off!

Long stop

FIRST WHORE. We are two big whores.

SECOND WHORE. Huge whores.

FIRST WHORE. Huge whores.

SECOND WHORE. We sell our bodies.

FIRST WHORE. For money.

SECOND WHORE. For money.

FIRST WHORE. We provide…

SECOND WHORE. Shelter.

FIRST WHORE. That's right. We provide shelter.

SECOND WHORE. And comfort.

FIRST WHORE. And comfort.

SECOND WHORE. And we love it.

FIRST WHORE. And our clients love us.

SECOND WHORE. We offer bliss.

FIRST WHORE. Yes! Bliss! Why didn't I think of that word?

SECOND WHORE. That's because you're a whore, dear.

FIRST WHORE. Thank you, and you're a whore too.

SECOND WHORE. Tonight we go to the theatre.

FIRST WHORE. Yes, our two clients are taking us out to the theatre.

SECOND WHORE. We are so sophisticated.

FIRST WHORE. We are the classiest whores in the world.

SECOND WHORE. We will sip champagne at the theatre.

FIRST WHORE. And we will eat caviar.

SECOND WHORE. Well, I don't know if they sell caviar at the theatre.

FIRST WHORE. Oh, I'm sure our clients will…

SECOND WHORE. Let's not call them that tonight. Tonight they're our friends.

FIRST WHORE. Yes. Tonight they're our friends. I'm sure our friends will bring caviar from their homes.

SECOND WHORE. Are they Russian?

FIRST WHORE. Well… They do have an accent of some sort.

SECOND WHORE. I bet they're Russian.

FIRST WHORE. Yeah, why not. Our Russian friends.

SECOND WHORE. I wonder what the theatre will be like.

FIRST WHORE. Oh, they have all sorts there.

SECOND WHORE. Will they have songs?

FIRST WHORE. I'm sure they will.

SECOND WHORE. What about deaths?

FIRST WHORE. Always. You can't have a good play without good deaths.

SECOND WHORE. I'm very excited.

FIRST WHORE. Yes. Me too.

SECOND WHORE. Two whores at the theatre. Now that's going to be interesting.

FIRST WHORE. Do you think anyone will look down on us?

SECOND WHORE. How can they? We are sophisticated. We're even wearing our most sophisticated outfits.

FIRST WHORE. Oh, Whore, I am happy.

SECOND WHORE. Oh, Whore, so am I.

FIRST WHORE. We are the luckiest whores in the world.

They start dancing

I can't wait for our Russian friends to arrive.

SECOND WHORE. With caviar.

FIRST WHORE. And champagne.

SECOND WHORE. And the tickets to the theatre.

FIRST WHORE. I'm full of anticipation.

SECOND WHORE. Me too, my sophisticated whore friend. Me too.

WIFE and HUSBAND enter

WIFE. Husband…

HUSBAND. Yes, Wife.

WIFE. Today I reached a decision.

HUSBAND. Well, Wife, I am happy that you reached a decision. You seemed to be missing something, and perhaps it was a decision.

WIFE. Oh, Husband. I am glad I married you. You are right. I was empty and missing something and this decision has filled my life with new meaning and hope. I was sitting at home so miserable, not knowing what I was feeling. I was in pain. Pain inside. Pain in my heart. I was so pained and so I pined. You pined for this, and I for what I miss.

HUSBAND. So what is the decision you so elatedly made? What are you missing?

WIFE. Right… well, I closed my eyes and focused on my pain. I retracted it and started to look for its birthplace. I made a shocking discovery – the pain originated from my womb. My womb was in pain. And then I realised what can cause such wombly pains. So I would like you to impregnate me!

Long stop

I would like you to…

HUSBAND. Yes. I… did hear what you said.

WIFE. You don't seem happy.

HUSBAND. I… I am happy! I must admit, Wife, I was scared for a moment, but I do see the light. A baby. That would be… rewarding.

WIFE. A little mini Husband or a little mini Wife for us to take care of.

HUSBAND. And nurture.

WIFE. And grow.

HUSBAND. And make into a perfect human being.

WIFE. Oh Husband, it might even be twins.

HUSBAND. Oh Wife, it might even be more.

WIFE. My vagina would not handle all that, Husband.

HUSBAND. You are right, Wife.

WIFE. Oh, husband. Shall we fornicate now?

HUSBAND. Why not. Let's fornicate now.

WIFE. I can't wait for your sperm to enter my egg.

HUSBAND and WIFE leave
CAPTAIN KYIL enters the stage holding a rifle

CAPTAIN KYIL. Oh, what kind of a soldier am I? I've been protecting all my life, yet I've never killed anyone. I wonder what it would feel like to kill. To take a person's life. And all the blood. The blood exiting the wounds. All those sad empty creatures. Blood oozing out of their holes. Blood emptying from their bodies. Kill them until they have no life. Oh, killing must be so much fun. Phil, do let me feel what it feels like to kill. For now, I will have to be satisfied with protecting the streets.

As CAPTAIN KYIL shouts, all the characters except PHIL enter the stage one by one

Ladies and Gentlemen, I am Captain Kyil and I am the protector of this town. Come out and listen to me! From now on there will be some ground rules. A curfew will come into place every evening at ten PM. Anyone seen out on the streets after that will be shot. Shot to kill. So don't leave your homes.

HUSBAND. But what if we must?

CAPTAIN KYIL. You never must.

HUSBAND. Sometimes we have to leave our house for our loves.

CAPTAIN KYIL. You do not have to leave for love!

HUSBAND. I refuse to accept that.

CAPTAIN KYIL. Then I refuse to keep you alive and I will be forced to use force.

WIFE. Come, Husband. Don't argue with Captain Kyil. You will live for love but not leave for love. Now let's get back inside and you can return to your rejoicement.

DOCTOR HIIL. Captain Kyil.

CAPTAIN KYIL. Yes, Doctor Hiil.

DOCTOR HIIL. I assume this curfew will not affect me, is that right?

CAPTAIN KYIL. Of course it will, Doctor Hiil.

DOCTOR HIIL. But what if I must go and treat a patient?

CAPTAIN KYIL. No one is to be ill after ten.

FATSO. You need not worry about me. I sleep at ten. You see, after my seven-course nightly meal at eight, I take a long bath… with bubbles. I smoke a large cigar, drink a glass – not too much, I'm not an alcoholic, after all – of Cognac and then by ten, I am always in bed. With my satin pajamas and silky sheets and hundreds of pillows. I am too fat to do anything else. Besides, sleeping is fun. I happily sleep Captain Kyil, you will not see me out of my house past the curfew.

CAPTAIN KYIL. That is excellent news, Fatso. You can all go back to your homes now!

They all return to their homes except for DOCTOR HIIL, FATSO and the WHORES

DOCTOR HIIL. Fatso...

FATSO. Yes, Doctor Hiil.

DOCTOR HIIL. I'm concerned about your size. You are very fat.

FATSO. I know, Doctor Hiil.

DOCTOR HIIL. Why are you so fat, Fatso?

FATSO. I... eat too much?

DOCTOR HIIL. Yes. Why else?

FATSO. Oh, do I have glandular problems?

DOCTOR HIIL. Possibly.

FATSO. Oh, I know. I don't exercise enough.

DOCTOR HIIL. Enough?

FATSO. At all.

DOCTOR HIIL. Yes.

FATSO. Are there any other reasons?

DOCTOR HIIL. Do you have a problem with over-indulgence?

FATSO. I don't think so. I over-indulge fairly easily.

DOCTOR HIIL. Fatso, you have to take better care of yourself otherwise Phil might smite you.

FATSO. And is that bad, Doctor Hiil?

DOCTOR HIIL. Very bad, Fatso. You do not want Phil to smite you.

FATSO. Right, Doctor Hiil. I will do what is needed of me not to be smitten.

DOCTOR HIIL. Smited.

FATSO. Smited.

DOCTOR HIIL. If you make sure you make amends, you may come out of it and survive.

FATSO. Oh, I want to survive, Doctor Hiil. I don't want to die. I'm still too young to die. I've not yet lived. I've not kissed a woman. I've not eaten pig's liver. I've not been to the jungles of America. I don't want to die.

DOCTOR HIIL. Then stop eating!

FATSO. But when I was born I was promised life. I was told that if I didn't eat – I would die. So I ate, and I drank and I pooped and I grew. Nobody told me that if I eat too much I would die as well. I was never given that warning. It's not fair. This world is steeped with such delicious food. Such tasty and appetising delicious sustaining, substantial, sufficient, satiating, satisfying, salivating, saturated food.

DOCTOR HIIL. I believe in you, Fatso! You can do it!

FATSO. Thank you, Doctor Hiil.

DOCTOR HIIL exits
FATSO starts walking in circles muttering words and punching the air
THE SUICIDER enters the stage and runs to FATSO

THE SUICIDER. Fatso, surely you have a piece of rope you can give me!

FATSO. And what would I do with a piece of rope?

THE SUICIDER. Oh, great disappointment. Thank you for failing.

FATSO. I'm very good at that.

THE SUICIDER. I'm better!

FATSO exits
THE SUICIDER knocks on HUSBAND and WIFE's door

HUSBAND. Yes?

THE SUICIDER. Husband, do you have a razor?

HUSBAND. I need it for my shaving.

THE SUICIDER. I promise to return it.

WIFE. Husband, who disturbs us again in the middle of fornication?

HUSBAND. The Suicider wants to shave.

WIFE. But now is not the time.

HUSBAND. I am sorry, I would love to give you my razor, but Wife is right, now is not the time. Goodbye

THE SUICIDER. Now is never the time. Another disappointment! How many more can I take? I have a fragile soul and every disappointment leads me closer and closer to despair. No. I will not give up. I will succeed.

THE SUICIDER exits

FIRST WHORE. They're late.

SECOND WHORE. Very late.

FIRST WHORE. Very late.

SECOND WHORE. We're looking forward to showing our friends the time of their lives.

FIRST WHORE. After they show us the time of ours.

SECOND WHORE. We will make them happy.

FIRST WHORE. They will make us happy.

SECOND WHORE. Everybody will be happy.

FIRST WHORE. Now we wait.

SECOND WHORE. We wait.

FIRST WHORE. For our two Russian friends.

SECOND WHORE. I wonder what they'll be wearing.

FIRST WHORE. I wonder if they will like what we're wearing.

Long stop

TOGETHER. Of course they will.

FIRST WHORE. We are so sophisticated.

SECOND WHORE. So sophisticated.

DOCTOR HIIL knocks on HUSBAND and WIFE's door

DOCTOR HIIL. Husband, Wife... I have some fantastic news.

WIFE. Oh, Husband, can it really be?

DOCTOR HIIL. Yes, Wife. It is. You're pregnant.

HUSBAND. Oh, Doctor Hiil. Thank you so much. You have excited us, pleased us and happilised us.

WIFE. Doctor Hiil, Husband does not lie. We are the happiest we've ever been.

HUSBAND. Even more.

WIFE. Even more.

DOCTOR HIIL. Well, Husband, well Wife. I am glad to be your Doctor today and to see you now, when you are at the happiest you've ever been.

HUSBAND. Even more.

WIFE. Even more!

HUSBAND and WIFE exit, leaving DOCTOR HIIL alone

DOCTOR HIIL. New life! How exciting. There is nothing more important in life than living, is there? As long as we're alive and healthy. Living sick is not living at all. If living is the most important thing, and being healthy is the only way to live. I should be the most valuable person on earth. And yet… I thought to myself, If I become a Doctor I'd save the world. Hiil will heal the ill. But everybody dies. I failed them all. All I end up with are sick and dead. Dead and sick. Corpses and failure. Failure and corpses. Oh, why did I waste my life like this? I feel sick from this success-less life. When the doctor is sick, what hope is there for anyone?

Long stop

No, Doctor Hiil, you mustn't give up! Perhaps people die, but hope must never die! Hope! There must be hope if there is to be happiness. I must fight for hopiness! Hiil, you will heal the ill.

Scene 2 – Monastery

SISTER FATHER is sitting next to a hospital bed on which THE SUICIDER is laying
SISTER FATHER is nursing THE SUICIDER back to health

SISTER FATHER. Now, that was a stupid thing to do, wasn't it?

THE SUICIDER. Was it?

SISTER FATHER. You didn't read the instructions properly.

THE SUICIDER. Didn't I?

SISTER FATHER. You weren't supposed to swallow all the pills.

THE SUICIDER. Weren't I?

SISTER FATHER. I'm afraid the doctors have had to pump your stomach.

THE SUICIDER. Have had they?

SISTER FATHER. So was this an accident?

THE SUICIDER. It was.

SISTER FATHER. Oh, thank Phil. For a moment there I thought that you attempted suicide.

THE SUICIDER. Yes, Sister Father. The accident is that I survived!

SISTER FATHER. Your survival is a miracle. You must be grateful and thank Phil.

THE SUICIDER. Phil failed me.

SISTER FATHER. How?

THE SUICIDER. By not letting me die.

SISTER FATHER. Suicide is an act of moral lowness and results in punishment.

THE SUICIDER. But it's punishment for me to survive. Are you saying that by trying to kill myself I get punished with survival? But… This would mean I could never kill myself. What horrible fate is Phil laying on someone whose only wish is to die? Phil, can you hear me?

THE SUICIDER gets up and rummages around looking for something, eventually finding a knife

Phil, look at this. I want to die.

THE SUICIDER sticks the knife - it's a toy knife and it breaks

What is this meant to be? You can't do that! That's not fair. So many innocent people die every day. So many people who don't want to die end up in the morgue. And here am I, a simple failure and all I want is to die, and you won't even give me that? Let me be noble. Allow me to pretend to be thoughtful and cry to the world "take me, instead of them". Let me jump and catch a bullet for someone. Let me push someone out of the road and fall in front of a bus. Why are you killing them and not me? This is not fair. It's not fair!

THE SUICIDER breaks down crying
SISTER FATHER starts consoling THE SUICIDER

SISTER FATHER. Phil works in mysterious ways.

Stop

Dear Suicider, for solidarity, I will dedicate my life to trying to die for others. Just so you won't feel alone.

THE SUICIDER gets up and storms out as FATSO enters

FATSO. Sister Father.

SISTER FATHER. Yes, Fatso.

FATSO. I need help.

SISTER FATHER. Well, I am here to help. I am help. How may I help you?

FATSO. Doctor Hiil said that if I eat again I would die.

SISTER FATHER. And what is the problem?

FATSO. I'm hungry.

SISTER FATHER. Fatso, we must give up these pleasures in order to be pure. We are all Phil's children and in order to receive love from Phil we must deny ourselves these gratuitous pleasures.

FATSO. Yes, I understand but… I'm hungry.

SISTER FATHER. Fatso, I'll tell you what I'll do. I will assist you.

FATSO. You will assist me, Sister Father?

SISTER FATHER. For solidarity, I will also starve and stop eating.

FATSO. You are a saint for starving and stopping eating to assist me for solidarity, Sister Father.

SISTER FATHER. Oh, please. It's part of my duty for serving Phil. From now on I will not eat anymore. I will will my will to behave.

FATSO. Thank you.

SISTER FATHER. All in a day's job, Fatso. All in a lifetime's calling.

SISTER FATHER leaves

FATSO. Excellent. From now on I will eat no more.

Stop

Oh, my stomach started talking to me. What is it that you're saying? I can't understand you under all those grumbles. You feel lonely. Yes. I understand. Fatso, do you want to be happy or healthy? To be me or not to be me? My flaws are what construct me and make me unique. For all my life you've been telling me to love the person I've become. Now you tell me I was wrong all along? Upon my deathbed, would I rather feel like a work of art or a happy soul? To deal and cope and float on a breeze or to thine own self be true?

A pregnant WIFE enters

Wife!

WIFE. Yes, Fatso!

FATSO. You are pregnant.

WIFE. I know, Fatso.

FATSO. Do you get… cravings?

WIFE. I do.

FATSO. Oh, wife. Would you tell me about your cravings?

WIFE. Of course.

FATSO sits on the floor and cradles into WIFE, like a child being told a bedtime story

Last night I woke up in the middle of the night wanting to eat olives.

FATSO. Green or black?

WIFE. Green, obviously. I wanted old green olives, but ended up having to make do with olive oil.

FATSO. Oil?

WIFE. Yes. I drank half a bottle of olive oil.

FATSO. Extra virgin?

WIFE. Of course, Fatso. Oh, you are sweet and innocent.

FATSO. Like a virgin?

WIFE. Like the finest extra virgin oil there is.

FATSO. What did you eat with the oil?

WIFE. Chocolate and rice and mousse with allspice.

FATSO. Tell me more.

WIFE. *(sings)*

Pork pies with whipped cream and topped with some cheese
Kidneys and honey from the finest bees
Chicken in seaweed with corn in a flan

Noodles in saffron with truffle sauce and naan
Forty kinds of chocolate with sardines on the side
Marmite fondue and a swan that just died
Pizza with breadcrumbs and apricot cheese
and finally a milkshake from spinach and peas
Pasta with baked beans and caramel sauce
Bacon ice cream and that's just the first course

FATSO. Thank you, Wife. You are kind.

WIFE. It's my pleasure, Fatso. It's my pleasure.

FATSO falls asleep
CHAIRMAN KESH enters and stands in the middle of the street looking at all the notes

CHAIRMAN KESH. I'm richer. My life is becoming more and more satisfying. Yet... I still feel like I can get more. I now have twenty notes, but surely twenty notes are not enough. I want more notes!

DOCTOR HIIL enters

Ahh, Doctor Hiil. You must want to buy something from me, right?

DOCTOR HIIL. What can someone like you have to sell that a person like me needs?

CHAIRMAN KESH. Shoes?

DOCTOR HIIL. Well I do must walk quite a lot in order to treat patients. But are they clean? Are they sterile? Are you sure they have no germs, bacterias or feline urine on them?

CHAIRMAN KESH. I am as sure as I am that felines urinate.

DOCTOR HIIL. In which case, I'll take them! How much do you want?

CHAIRMAN KESH. How much do you think is fair for these beautiful shoes?

DOCTOR HIIL. Thirty Notes?

CHAIRMAN KESH. I agree!

CHAIRMAN KESH gives DOCTOR HIIL a pair of shoes in exchange for thirty notes
DOCTOR HIIL exits

This is fun! What else can I sell? Wife, Fatso, would you like to buy anything from me?

WIFE. Do you have maternity clothes?

CHAIRMAN KESH. Why would I have maternity clothes?

WIFE. Chairman Kesh, you are of no use to me. Good day!

WIFE exits
FATSO wakes up

FATSO. Oh, Chairman Kesh, what did you have for breakfast this morning?

CHAIRMAN KESH. If I tell you, will you pay me for it?

FATSO. How much?

CHAIRMAN KESH. How much do you think is fair for this beautiful telling?

FATSO. Forty notes.

FATSO pays CHAIRMAN KESH

CHAIRMAN KESH. Oh, hurrah! Well, I ate three eggs. I always eat three eggs. Every morning I eat three eggs. One boiled, one scrambled and one sunny side up.

FATSO. Tell me more, Chairman Kesh.

CHAIRMAN KESH. The eggs are reared in the best farms in the country. Only the finest chickens lay my eggs.

FATSO. Chicken… Tell me more about the chicken.

CHAIRMAN KESH. It's an Indian chicken. They lay only the smoothest, creamiest eggs. So delicious, your tongue melts as you eat them.

FATSO. Tongue… Cream… Tongue in cream… Do you put any seasoning on it?

CHAIRMAN KESH. Salt, of course.

FATSO. I love salt.

CHAIRMAN KESH. Would you like to buy some eggs from me?

FATSO. I wish I could, but I am not allowed. The cholesterol!

CAPTAIN KYIL approaches

CAPTAIN KYIL. It's late. It's almost curfew time. You must go home.

FATSO. Yes, Captain Kyil.

FATSO exits

CHAIRMAN KESH. Before I go, would you like to buy my trousers?

CAPTAIN KYIL. Well, they are very nice trousers. How much would you like for them?

CHAIRMAN KESH. How much do you think is fair for these beautiful trousers?

CAPTAIN KYIL. Sixty notes.

CHAIRMAN KESH. Oh, hurrah! I'm now going to have one hundred and fifty notes. I am rich.

CHAIRMAN KESH exchanges the trousers for Sixty notes

CAPTAIN KYIL. Now you must go home.

CHAIRMAN KESH. Straightaway.

CAPTAIN KYIL exits

I have one hundred notes and yet, I still don't feel satisfied. I want more.

SISTER FATHER enters

SISTER FATHER. Excuse me.

CHAIRMAN KESH. Yes.

SISTER FATHER. You're naked.

CHAIRMAN KESH. I am.

SISTER FATHER. Why are you naked?

CHAIRMAN KESH. I sold all my clothes.

SISTER FATHER. Oh, you poor poor creature. For solidarity, please, allow me to give up my clothes for you.

CHAIRMAN KESH. You will give me your clothes?

SISTER FATHER. Yes.

CHAIRMAN KESH. How much do you want for them?

SISTER FATHER. Nothing. I will give them to you for free.

CHAIRMAN KESH. What an odd business proposal. I'll take it.

SISTER FATHER undresses and hands the clothes to CHAIRMAN KESH who exits joyfully

SISTER FATHER. Oh, Great Phil. Thank you for helping me fulfil my duty. Giving up things blissfulifies me. I want to give up more. I want to please you more. I will do anything for your approval, Phil. Anything. I am your wife, your husband, your mistress, your butler and your maid. I am your kinky little bit on the side and the girl next door. For solidarity, I will end all worldly pleasures for you. I am yours for eternity, Phil. Take me and do with me as you will, Phil. Fill me with your love, Phil. Fill me with your will, Phil. Fill me, Phil. Fulfil me, Phil. Fulfil me fully, Phil.

SISTER FATHER faints from excitement
WIFE approaches HUSBAND holding a baby

WIFE. Husband…

HUSBAND. Yes, Wife.

WIFE. After many long hours of labour, I would like to introduce you to our baby.

HUSBAND. Our very own baby.

WIFE. A little Husband, a little Wife.

HUSBAND. Someone to love us.

WIFE. Someone to take care of us when we are old.

HUSBAND. Someone to share our education with.

WIFE. Someone to continue our lineage.

HUSBAND. Someone to take care of.

WIFE. To feed.

HUSBAND. And to cuddle.

WIFE. And to mollycoddle.

HUSBAND. And to wash.

WIFE. And to hug.

HUSBAND. And to kiss.

WIFE. And to love.

HUSBAND. You can love me.

WIFE. I do. We both do. We will all love each other. And smell the baby. Doesn't our child smell magnificent?

HUSBAND. Oh, yes. What a wonderful smell. Is that what your insides smell of?

WIFE. It must be.

HUSBAND. Oh, I am happy.

WIFE. So am I.

HUSBAND. This is the most beautiful baby in the world.

HUSBAND and WIFE exit

FIRST WHORE. We were stood up.

SECOND WHORE. We looked so beautiful, didn't we?

FIRST WHORE. Yes, we did. We looked beautiful.

SECOND WHORE. And we stood outside the theatre.

FIRST WHORE. Everyone was looking at us.

SECOND WHORE. They were jealous.

FIRST WHORE. Of our sophisticated outfits.

SECOND WHORE. We looked so beautiful.

Stop

Why didn't they come?

FIRST WHORE. We had no champagne.

SECOND WHORE. We had no caviar.

FIRST WHORE. And we were all alone.

SECOND WHORE. All alone.

FIRST WHORE. My dear Whore…

SECOND WHORE. Yes, my dearer Whore?

FIRST WHORE. I feel cheap.

SECOND WHORE. I know you do... I know.

Scene 3 - Bakery

BAKER stands alone in the bakery
After a few moments BAKER takes out a piece of paper and pen and starts writing a will

BAKER. Oh, woe me. I've been baking for so many years, yet I am still an insignificant, tiny baker, working in an insignificant, tiny bakery, living in an insignificant tiny town baking insignificant tiny goods for insignificant tiny clients who think insignificantly and tinily of my work. When I was young, I was a prodigy. A genius. Destined to bake the most incredible food. And when I entered baking school all eyes opened wide and pallets climaxed, all mouths gasped. And now. Now I am in woe. Time's lost its track and so have I. I sit now and write this will – when I die, I want my epitaph to say, "He had great potential". What did I do wrong? Why is my cheek being slapped so sillily? A master baker – master of nothing. If a cake is baked in the middle of a forest and nobody eats it, does it still exist? Do I have a point to exist? I wanted to be pointed to the nearest point, but instead was shown the backdoor. Goodbye cakes and waffles and biscuits and buns.

FATSO walks into the Bakery

FATSO. Excuse me, I used to be thin.

BAKER. *(angrily)* And I used to be young. We all have to deal with disappointments. We all must cope with our bodies never quite being as they were. I used to be young, and now all I have are wrinkles. Wrinkles and grey hairs. So why should I care about you being thin? Do you care about me being young?

FATSO. You don't understand. You are the reason to my fatity.

BAKER. Me?

FATSO. You bake such delicious cakes in the shop and the smell coming from the oven teases me, every morning when I wake up.

Long stop

I used to be thin.

BAKER. Well, my overly-calorized friend, I can assure you that it was never my intention to sadden or fatten you. Although it does give me a great feeling of joy and consummation to see your calories and know they were my creation. Am I allowed to touch them?

FATSO. I… I guess so.

BAKER. Oh, wonderful folding. Beautiful bulging and the spillage… oh, the spillage. You are like a work of art – so beautiful. So… full. And this is all me?

FATSO. Well, I have been known to eat other things?

BAKER. Other things? How many other things?

FATSO. Not as many as yours. See this piece of extra skin surrounding a large piece of fat?

BAKER. I see it.

FATSO. That is from your triple-chocolate obsession cake.

BAKER. The one with the white chocolate filling?

FATSO. The one with the white chocolate filling!

BAKER. And what about this lovely piece of thigh?

FATSO. This is from the indulgent strawberry and treacle cream cake.

BAKER. The one in which the strawberries are made of sugar...

FATSO. That is precisely the one.

CAPTAIN KYIL enters the Bakery

CAPTAIN KYIL. Baker, Fatso...

BOTH. Yes, Captain Kyil.

CAPTAIN KYIL. Are you aware of the curfew?

BOTH. Yes, Captain Kyil.

CAPTAIN KYIL. Good.

BAKER. Would you like a muffin, Captain Kyil?

CAPTAIN KYIL. Wow. You just offered me a muffin. I did not expect such kindness from you town-folk. I don't like muffins, so I'll refuse your offer, but I am gobsmacked by your kindness. I come to do my duty. I come to work and do what is required of me, and in return – in selfless return, might I add – you shower me with offers of muffins. Baker, will you be my best friend?

BAKER. I would be honoured.

CAPTAIN KYIL. Well, I must go now. The streets won't protect themselves, you know. *(excited)* I have a friend!

CAPTAIN KYILL exits as HUSBAND enters and stands in a queue behind FATSO

BAKER. Husband, congratulations.

FATSO. Yes, such splendid news.

HUSBAND. Well, perhaps…

FATSO. A child.

BAKER. You have a child.

HUSBAND. Yes. I do.

BAKER. From now on you're a family.

HUSBAND. Well, yes…

BAKER. You don't seem sure.

HUSBAND. Well, I don't know if I want a child.

FATSO. It wasn't our doing.

HUSBAND. I never asked for a child. I asked for a wife. I got a wife. I got Wife. Wife is my wife. I didn't ask for Child to be my child. Now I have a wife and a child. I don't think I want either of them.

FATSO. Poppycock! I'm sure when you look at the child you feel joy!

HUSBAND. Come to think of it, when I look at the child's eyes the child looks back at me with disappointment. I can never live up to the fantasy of the father the child wants. I am a husband. Not a father. The child will only grow to hate me, and the wife… well, she will grow to resent me. A hating child and a resenting wife. I never asked for either of them.

FATSO. Oh, Husband, you're just scared.

HUSBAND. I am not scared! I am mean. I mean, I am a mean man. I should run away before they suffer. I am doing them a favour. That's right. Doing them a favour. This way the child will never have to deal with the disappointment of discovering what a failure his father is. Oh, I don't know what to do, Fatso!

HUSBAND starts crying and hugs FATSO

BAKER. Well, Fatso, I must feed you.

FATSO. Oh, I can't lie – that will cause me tremendous joy, yet sadness at the same time. I feel conflicted.

BAKER. Eat. Food always solves conflicts.

FATSO. Doctor Hiil said I needed a diet.

BAKER. But Fatso, there is no joy in dietetic food, is there.

FATSO. Dietetic, diabetic diabolic food.

BAKER. Fatso, look at these cakes. Look at these little bundles of joy. Think of the smiles they will create once entering your lips. Imagine the memories. Imagine the stories you will tell your grandchildren. Imagine what you can do with these gifts of carbohydrates in your body.

FATSO. Fatso, this is your moment... I will have a piece of your finest cake, Baker.

PHIL enters and hits FATSO on the heart
FATSO collapses on the floor on top of HUSBAND, killing him

BAKER. A heart attack? In my bakery? And not one, but two bodies. What will people say? What do I do with the bodies?

BAKER sits on the two bodies thinking

Oh, my beautiful stretchy-skinned Fatso. Your heart stopped in the prime of your existence. Just as you were about to add some more scope to your breadthy body.

BAKER looks around to check if anyone is coming and starts juggling FATSO's breasts

I never had the chance to juggle and jiggle your breasts. Luscious! Splendid! Marvelous! Fatso, words escape me. My poor, poor, Fatso. Perfect in every curve. My real true work of art. Fatso, your death will not be in vain! I will find another canvas to feed. I will find another hungry stretch of fabric!

BAKER runs out
PHIL escorts HUSBAND and FATSO out through the door marked 'Phil'

Scene 4 – Home

SISTER FATHER approaches WIFE who is holding the baby

SISTER FATHER. Wife…

WIFE. Yes, Sister Father.

SISTER FATHER. I'm afraid I have some terrible news.

WIFE. Terrible news?

SISTER FATHER. Yes.

WIFE. Should I sit down?

SISTER FATHER. If you wish.

WIFE sits down

WIFE. Should I get myself a glass of water?

SISTER FATHER. If you wish.

WIFE gets a gluss of water

WIFE. Should I place pillows on the floor in case I faint?

SISTER FATHER. If you wish.

WIFE takes a pillow and places it on the front near her

WIFE. Should I give you my baby so I don't drop it?

SISTER FATHER. If you wish.

WIFE gives SISTER FATHER the baby

WIFE. Should I… hear what you have to say?

SISTER FATHER. Yes.

WIFE. Please, Sister Father, tell me.

SISTER FATHER. I'm afraid your husband died.

WIFE. Did he?

SISTER FATHER. He did. He died.

WIFE. I understand.

Stop

So now I'm alone?

SISTER FATHER. Now you're alone.

WIFE. A lonely woman.

SISTER FATHER. You have your baby.

WIFE. Yes. My baby. My little chicken. But my husband. My husband is dead. I had a husband. I married Husband so he could father my child. And Husband gave me Child. And now I have no husband but I have a child.

Stop

(plainly) oh, how will we afford to eat?

SISTER FATHER. That's a problem.

WIFE. And the rent?

SISTER FATHER. Another problem.

WIFE. Sister Father, have you any solutions?

SISTER FATHER. I do not.

WIFE. Sister Father, you are very cruel to have told me such horrible news.

SISTER FATHER. And I'm sorry to have to be the bearer of such horrible news. I will now take a vow of silence so that I never cause such hurt to anyone.

WIFE. That might be wise, Sister Father.

No response

Sister Father...

No response

Sister Father...

No response

Sister Father...

No response

Sister Father...

No response

Sister Father...

SISTER FATHER walks out broken and silent
WIFE walks over to the baby's cot
As she sings the song, she slowly dies

WIFE. *(sings) My dearest child you will now die*
You must be killed and so must I
My dearest child please don't be scared
For soon my dear we'll both be dead
My dearest child so young in the days
And still this world is quite a haze
My dearest child your death is dumb
But I right now am feeling numb

My dearest child the gas will run
We'll soon be free, and just have fun
My dearest child forgive your mother
That you, so young, she has to smother
Yes, dearest child I'm feeling unwell
My mental world is constant hell
I'd rather die and burn for eternity
Than live with you post this maternity
My dearest child your father waits
We'll join him at the pearly gates
My dearest child, a farewell kiss
To seal your life with total bliss

As the song fades out, PHIL enters and escorts WIFE out through the door marked 'Phil'

Scene 5 – End Of The Road

SISTER FATHER sits on stage in the middle of the road
BAKER enters

BAKER. *(shouts)* Someone eat my bread! *(sees Sister Father)* Sister Father, you will eat my bread!

No response

Sister Father…

No response

Sister Father…

No response

Sister Father…

No response

Oh, wonderful. Here. Bread! Bread! Bread!

BAKER starts feeding SISTER FATHER bread
SISTER FATHER does not resist
Just as SISTER FATHER is about to choke, CAPTAIN KYIL enters

CAPTAIN KYIL. What are you doing outside? It's past the curfew. Go home! Baker, what are you doing?

BAKER. Oh, Captain Kyil. What an amazing sensation. Soon Sister Father will be fat like Fatso was.

CAPTAIN KYIL. Baker, you have to stop. You can't keep on sticking buns in Sister Father's mouth. Enough, Baker! Shoo! Shoo!

BAKER exits

CAPTAIN KYIL. Now, Sister Father, you can't be here either…

No response

Sister Father…

No response

Sister Father…

No response

Sister Father...

No response

Sister Father, it's past the curfew, if you don't move I will have to kill you. It is my duty and my job to kill you.

No response

Oh, don't make me kill you, Sister Father. What if it's not as exciting as I had thought? I'm scared. Unless of course you fight back. Yes. You can overpower me. Perhaps you can kidnap me. Take me hostage. Keep me for ransom. Be violent with me. Grab me by the hair. Like this. Then strangle me. Like this. And grab hold of my arm. Like this. Stick my head in the dirt. Like this. Make me beg for forgiveness. Like this. Help! Please release me. I beg you! Maybe even rape me. Like this. Spit on me. Like this. Fight back. Fight me. Kill me before I kill you.

No response

Sister Father, I will ask you one last time, to please get up and go before I kill you.

Stop

In which case, I have no other choice. In the name of the army, I shoot you for violating the curfew.

CAPTAIN KYIL shoots SISTER FATHER who falls on the floor dead

Wow. So easy to kill someone. I shoot – bang. They fall down – boom. Bang – Boom – Bang – Boom – Bang – Boom – Bang – Boom. I am now a killer!

THE SUICIDER enters crying

You are not allowed to be here. It's past the curfew.

THE SUICIDER. I don't care! I don't care! I don't care! You see, I can't die. Nothing can kill me. I just drank a whole bottle of acid and all I got from it was indigestion. I sat in a building as it was burning and got a tan. I am immortal. I don't care about any curfews. So please, if you don't mind, I still have a terrible headache from trying to shoot myself.

CAPTAIN KYIL. But… I have a rifle.

THE SUICIDER. Come on then. Do your worst! I dare you.

CAPTAIN KYIL. In the name of the army, I shoot you for violating the curfew.

CAPTAIN KYIL shoots THE SUICIDER

THE SUICIDER. You shot me… I… I'm dying now? Is this dying? Oh, that is sensational. Yes. I feel life leaving my body. This is an incredible feeling. I will finally reach death. I finally succeeded in killing myself.

CAPTAIN KYIL. But you didn't kill yourself. I shot you.

THE SUICIDER. What? I've been murdered. I'm a murder victim. I'm not a suicide anymore. I wanted to kill myself. I thought I wanted to die, but I don't want to die. It wasn't that at all.

CAPTAIN KYIL. You're whining for no reason. It's all exactly the same.

THE SUICIDER. No... No! Listen to me. Let me kill myself. Give me your rifle. Allow me to shoot myself quickly before I die. I beg of you.

CAPTAIN KYIL. I can't.

THE SUICIDER. I'm running out of time. Please. I must be allowed to do it. Just before all life exits my body. Surely it's my human right to kill myself?

CAPTAIN KYIL. I don't know anything about human rights.

THE SUICIDER starts running around the room looking for something with which to commit suicide
As the speech continues, THE SUICIDER gradually becomes weaker and weaker

THE SUICIDER. I'm dying. It's going. It's finally happening. My life is almost completely out. And I will die with no dignity. I will die a poor mere murder victim. A collateral of war. An army surplus. Just another anonymous name in a mass grave of human enigma. I will be nothing. Nothing. A whole life lived for nothing. This is not fair. I am quite very cross about this. Quite very cross indeed. I would like to complain to your commander, please. Phil! I need Phil! Phil will heal so I could kill myself!

THE SUICIDER exits through the door marked 'Phil', with a final breath

CAPTAIN KYIL. Wow. Bang – Boom – Bang – Boom – Bang – Boom – Bang – Boom. My second kill-ey. How delicious! *(shouts)* There is a curfew and nobody is to stay outside!

BAKER enters

BAKER. I must feed you!

Without looking, CAPTAIN KYIL shoots BAKER who falls dead on the floor

CAPTAIN KYIL. Oh, it's you. My best friend. Why are you out after the curfew? Bang – Boom. Bang – Boom. This doesn't feel as nice. I killed my friend. I didn't want to kill friends. I wanted to kill the enemy.

Stop

I feel remorse. Remorse is not a feeling a soldier should feel. Bang – Boom. Friend dead.

Stop

I am very sad now.

Stop

I am… Bang… Boom… Bang… Boom… Bang…

CAPTAIN KYIL commits suicide with the rifle and collapses dead on the floor
PHIL enters and escorts all three bodies out through the door marked 'Phil'
CHAIRMAN KESH enters

CHAIRMAN KESH. I've sold all my clothes and all of Sister Father's clothes. I now have two hundred notes. I must be the richest person in the world. I am content. Satisfied. I can't be any more satisfied than this… except… that I would like to have four hundred notes now. And then I'll be content. Four hundred notes will make me content. Unless of course I can then get eight hundred notes. Or sixteen hundred notes. Or thirty two hundred notes, or sixty four hundred notes, or one hundred and twenty eight hundred notes… Curse you, mathematics for creating a never-ending table of accumulation. Two hundred and fifty six hundred notes, or five hundred and twelve hundred notes… Where is the end? One thousand and twenty four hundred notes… there is no end. Two thousand and forty eight hundred notes. Somebody find the limit! Four thousand and ninety six hundred notes… I… There is no end, is there? There is no end! Eight thousand one hundred and ninety two hundred notes. There is no end! Sixteen thousand three hundred and eighty four hundred notes. Thirty two thousand seven hundred and sixty eight hundred notes. Sixty five thousand five hundred and thirty six hundred notes.
One hundred and thirty one thousand and seventy two hundred notes. Two hundred and sixty two thousand one

hundred and forty four hundred notes. Five hundred and twenty four thousand two hundred and eighty eight hundred notes.

FIRST WHORE. Will you just shut up?

SECOND WHORE. Yeah! Shut up and piss off!

CHAIRMAN KESH. One million forty eight thousand five hundred and seventy six hundred notes. Two million eighty seven thousand one hundred and fifty two hundred notes…

CHAIRMAN KESH continues multiplying as FIRST WHORE goes to knock on the door marked 'Phil'
PHIL opens

PHIL. Yes?

FIRST WHORE. Can you please shut Chairman Kesh up? I'm getting such a headache from these ramblings!

SECOND WHORE. Yeah! Me too!

PHIL. Sure…

PHIL escorts CHAIRMAN KESH out through the door marked 'Phil'

FIRST WHORE. That's much better! Isn't it much better?

SECOND WHORE. Yes. Much better.

FIRST WHORE. You know, I'm glad we didn't go to the theatre.

SECOND WHORE. I'm gladder.

FIRST WHORE. I bet it was a boring show, anyway.

SECOND WHORE. The songs were probably too simple.

FIRST WHORE. And the deaths were probably predictable.

SECOND WHORE. And the villain probably got no comeuppance.

FIRST WHORE. And they were probably just talking and talking and talking and nothing actually happened. Pretentious rhetoric.

SECOND WHORE. Rhetoric pretentiousness.

FIRST WHORE. Yes.

SECOND WHORE. I wonder if any of our clients were in it. We sometimes do actors.

FIRST WHORE. Do you remember our last client?

SECOND WHORE. The one that both of us did?

FIRST WHORE. Together.

SECOND WHORE. We sometimes do that.

FIRST WHORE. He came to us with a lot of money and told us he wanted us to…

SECOND WHORE. Pleasure each other.

FIRST WHORE. He sat and watched. And didn't even touch himself.

SECOND WHORE. He smoked a cigar and drank Whisky.

FIRST WHORE. And looked.

SECOND WHORE. Whilst we…

FIRST WHORE. Did it.

Stop

SECOND WHORE. I never understood him.

FIRST WHORE. He didn't even touch himself.

SECOND WHORE. I mean, why pay that much for whores and not pleasure yourself?

FIRST WHORE. I once had a client too.

SECOND WHORE. Alone.

FIRST WHORE. Yes.

SECOND WHORE. We also do that.

FIRST WHORE. We had so much sex.

SECOND WHORE. And what happened in the end?

FIRST WHORE. Nothing.

SECOND WHORE. You mean…

FIRST WHORE. Yes. Nothing!

SECOND WHORE. How unsatisfying.

FIRST WHORE. I got paid.

SECOND WHORE. Obviously, but for the client…

FIRST WHORE. I mean, we are in the business of giving pleasure.

SECOND WHORE. What is the point of going on the journey if you don't reach your destination?

Long Stop

FIRST WHORE. Whore?

SECOND WHORE. Yes…

FIRST WHORE. What is our destination?

SECOND WHORE. It is…

Stop

I don't know.

FIRST WHORE. How many clients must we fulfil? How many clients must we feel? How many clients must we fill?

SECOND WHORE. I… I don't know.

Very long Stop

FIRST WHORE. Whore, will you dance with me?

The TWO WHORES dance a dance of despair
After a few moments DOCTOR HIIL enters

DOCTOR HIIL. I've created a pill. Doctor Hiil's pill will heal the ill, thank Phil. I managed to find a way to save the world. I am exultant. I succeeded in successing my sickly and successless life. I can now cure everybody.

SECOND WHORE. Dead! Everybody is dead.

DOCTOR HIIL. Oh. Why?

SECOND WHORE. Phil!

FIRST WHORE. I'm sorry for your loss.

DOCTOR HIIL. Yes. A loss is indeed something to be sorry for.

SECOND WHORE. Do you want more pity?

DOCTOR HIIL. Thank you.

THE WHORES come and pat DOCTOR HIIL on the head

BOTH WHORES. There there! We pity you!

DOCTOR HIIL. Thank you. Your words are encouraging. So I am the last living person alive. I guess I won. Oh, but… I have nobody to heal?

SECOND WHORE. I'm afraid not.

DOCTOR HIIL sits full of despair

FIRST WHORE. The day is done.

SECOND WHORE. The clients are satisfied.

FIRST WHORE. The bed sheets have been washed.

SECOND WHORE. The bodies have been cleaned.

FIRST WHORE. Money was exchanged.

SECOND WHORE. Money was counted.

FIRST WHORE. Money was deposited.

SECOND WHORE. Money was spent.

FIRST WHORE. And now we can go to sleep.

SECOND WHORE. In our beautiful sophisticated pajamas.

FIRST WHORE. And start it all again tomorrow.

SECOND WHORE. Satisfy some more people?

FIRST WHORE. Satisfy some more people!

Long stop

SECOND WHORE. Whore, I'm tired.

FIRST WHORE. Me too.

SECOND WHORE. I've had enough.

FIRST WHORE. Shall we give up and join Phil?

SECOND WHORE. Perhaps.

THE WHORES start walking towards the door marked 'Phil'
DOCTOR HIIL notices them

DOCTOR HIIL. You can just go and join Phil?

SECOND WHORE. Oh, yes.

DOCTOR HIIL. Can I join you?

As they open the door, we see all the dead characters squeezed in a tiny room - they are all shouting
THE WHORES and DOCTOR HIIL try to squeeze in, as the door revolves and we are in PHIL's room

Scene 6 – Phil's

PHIL sits on a high chair
All the other characters are shouting and trying to get some attention angrily
There is a lot of noise

I don't understand.
Why am I here?
I've had a few more years in me.
I've been very good.
It's not fair. I said it's not fair.
Phil, I demand you reconsider.
Phil, if you just hear me out.

Very calmly PHIL raises the right hand - the room turns silent
Phil points at HUSBAND

HUSBAND. Thank you, Phil. I guess what I want to know is why me? Why now? I finally found love. I finally found responsibility. I have a reason to run, finally.

DOCTOR HIIL. And I finally managed to find a cure to all diseases, I think that trumps over love and responsibility any day.

HUSBAND. Shut up, Doctor Hiil. It's my turn to talk, isn't it, Phil?

PHIL nods

I think I should have been given at least a few more years.

WIFE. May I add something, Phil?

HUSBAND. *(explains)* She's my wife. We share the same voice.

PHIL nods

WIFE. I have waited my entire life to bring a child to the world, and I didn't even get to breast-feed it. Or to take care of it or to cuddle it or to mollycoddle it or to wash it or to nurse it or to hug it or to kiss it or to love it. I went through labour for nothing. Why did I have to go through it all only to end it all?

HUSBAND. You ended it all?

WIFE. I had to.

HUSBAND. So who's taking care of Child?

As HUSBAND realises the fate of the baby, he runs to the corner
WIFE follows him trying to console and explain

SISTER FATHER. I dedicated every waking moment to you, Phil. Why have you ignored me since I've arrived?

PHIL ignores SISTER FATHER and points at THE SUICIDER

THE SUICIDER. I always thought death was what I wanted, but it wasn't. It wasn't at all. I didn't want to die. I wanted to kill myself.

DOCTOR HIIL. It's all the same. You're whining for no reason. Why did I waste my life on people like you? *(points at FATSO)* and on people like you.

FATSO. I'm hungry! I'm always hungry! Why am I always hungry?

BAKER. You are so beautiful. At least I get to look at you for the rest of eternity.

PHIL, upon hearing BAKER's last comment gets up and turns FATSO and BAKER around so that they sit facing opposite ways
CHAIRMAN KESH approaches PHIL quietly

CHAIRMAN KESH. Phil, I'm sorry to bother you. I don't want much from you. I was wondering if I might please go back for one moment to collect the money I left on the street. I will be back instantly.

FIRST WHORE. Damn it! My heel broke!

SECOND WHORE. I told you not to wear these shoes!

PHIL walks to CAPTAIN KYIL, staring intensely into CAPTAIN KYIL's eyes

PHIL. You look sad. You should be glad.

CAPTAIN KYIL. I didn't save the world, and killing wasn't fun. Nothing will make me very glad.

PHIL. But you should all be glad. You are all with me now for eternity.

Long stop
Everybody starts shouting again angrily at PHIL who goes back to sit on the chair

Be quiet! I heard enough. Do you all remember the first chapter of the Book of Phil?

ALL. Yes.

PHIL. Recite it, please.

ALL. Phil woke up one day to find
That all existence is in the mind
Phil was lonely and prepared
To make a world out from the voices he heard
So that Phil wouldn't be alone
And have companions for which to moan
So Phil decided that it's time
To bring to life the dirt and grime
And Phil created men and pigs
And trees and lice and rocks and figs
Then Phil looked at them with a smile
And found out that they were hostile
And now we all live down below
And Phil protects us with a glow

PHIL. Precisely.

Long Stop

BAKER. Uhm, precisely what exactly, Phil?

PHIL. You were the biggest disappointment of them all.

Stop

WIFE. So?

PHIL. So, this is the way it is.

Stop

CAPTAIN KYIL. And what happens to us now?

PHIL. Nothing. You sit here for eternity and look at me with your disappointed eyes.

DOCTOR HIIL. That's it?

PHIL. That's it.

FIRST WHORE. Sorry, Phil, but I broke my heel. Can you please fix it!

PHIL. Silence!

Stop

SECOND WHORE. So we just sit here?

PHIL. Exactly.

HUSBAND. For eternity?

PHIL. Yes!

FATSO. And can we talk to each other?

PHIL. No.

CHAIRMAN KESH. Can we talk to you?

PHIL. No. Now be quiet. Everybody be quiet.

Long Stop

Good.

Lights go down as all sit silently and PHIL smiles

BLACKOUT

ACT TWO
Scene 1 – Phil's

An eternity later
The characters except WIFE are sitting on stage in the exact same positions as they were at the end of Act One, silent and terrified
PHIL sits looking paranoid
Eventually, PHIL stands up, observes everything and exits the room
First up is HUSBAND, going to see if PHIL's gone

HUSBAND. Phil's Gone.

BAKER. *(now blind)* Fatso, come to me.

FATSO gets up and walks to BAKER, taking BAKER's hands and placing them on the belly

Fatso, you've lost another gram. It's a bite of a croissant, isn't it? Another gram, another bite, a little less folding.

FATSO hugs BAKER tenderly as husband sits on PHIL's chair

FIRST WHORE. Husband, get off the chair. You are such a fool. Every day you annoy Phil and every day Phil punishes you.

SECOND WHORE. First Phil muted your wife.

FIRST WHORE. Then Phil cut off her limbs.

SECOND WHORE. Then Phil sent her to relive her death for all eternity, no?

FIRST WHORE. And worse of all, Phil still hasn't fixed my shoe. How much limping can I take?!

FATSO. And he blinded my Baker...

BAKER. I deserved it. I was greedy.

CAPTAIN KYIL. Nobody deserves it.

HUSBAND. I'm bored. And I miss Wife so very much. I keep thinking about her poor tortured soul. My poor muted, limb-less, suffocating Wife.

HUSBAND gets off the chair

THE SUICIDER. You miss Wife, and I miss life.

CHAIRMAN KESH. How long has it been now, anyway?

HUSBAND. It's been an eternity.

FIRST WHORE. That seems very long.

SECOND WHORE. Very long indeed.

HUSBAND. Shall we say something?

BAKER. Say something?

HUSBAND. Perhaps if we ask Phil nicely, we would be returned again.

FATSO. And what if Phil lets us down by refusing to let us down?

HUSBAND. Oh… I don't know.

THE SUICIDER. A mutiny!

CHAIRMAN KESH. Don't be ridiculous. Phil is much stronger than us.

FATSO. Phil is far more powerful.

THE SUICIDER. But there are so many of us.

HUSBAND. We must all be in this together, though.

DOCTOR HIIL. What's the worst that can happen? I'm completely useless here anyway. None of you need me.

THE SUICIDER. Captain Kyil?

CAPTAIN KYIL. I will not take part.

THE SUICIDER. Why not?

CAPTAIN KYIL. I don't want to fight Phil. I don't want to fight anyone. I can't anymore…

HUSBAND. Of course you can.

CAPTAIN KYIL. No. *(starts crying)* Even the thought of killing makes me sick. My stomach turns as I imagine all the blood. The blood exiting the wounds. All those poor souls. All those sad empty creatures. Blood oozing out of their holes. Blood emptying from their bodies. Poor little creatures. I'm sorry for killing you. I'm sorry for killing all of you.

Long stop

HUSBAND. Right…

THE SUICIDER. Uhm… I'm sure we can manage without Captain Kyil too.

HUSBAND. Sister Father?

FIRST WHORE. Leave her alone. She won't talk to any of us.

SECOND WHORE. We're not good enough for you, eh, Sister Father?

FIRST WHORE. We're too dirty!

SECOND WHORE. Too filthy!

FIRST WHORE. Too common!

SECOND WHORE. Poor you. Stuck here for eternity with all of us.

FIRST WHORE. I'm horny, Sister Father. Don't you want to have some fun?

SECOND WHORE. *(to the First Whore)* No sex!

FIRST WHORE. *(to the Second Whore)* No… no satisfaction!

SECOND WHORE. Whore, do you remember the days of frivolousness?

FIRST WHORE. I remember them too well.

SECOND WHORE. We were good, weren't we?

FIRST WHORE. Oh, we were. We were excellent.

HUSBAND. Enough! Chairman Kesh, will you take part?

CHAIRMAN KESH. How much do you think is fair for this beautiful taking part?

HUSBAND. How many times can we tell you that we have no money here? No possessions. Nothing. What do you want from us?

CHAIRMAN KESH. Just a note. One note. That's all I'm asking for.

FATSO. We need to be quick. Phil's returning.

CAPTAIN KYIL. What do we do now?

HUSBAND. I don't know. I really don't know.

They all run around like headless chickens
PHIL enters and they all stop frozen in their places – terrified

PHIL. You've moved.

Stop

All of you moved. What's going on here? Why have you all moved? You know you're not allowed to move. You mustn't move. I leave – you move? Had I wanted you to move, I would have moved you. Or at the very least, I would have told you to move. You cannot move when I leave just because I left.

SISTER FATHER approaches PHIL

SISTER FATHER. Phil, I need to tell you something. It's very important.

PHIL ignores SISTER FATHER who gets angry
DOCTOR HIIL approaches PHIL

DOCTOR HIIL. Oh, great Phil. I am very sorry to disturb you. I know we are not allowed to talk, and I apologise for this inconvenience and I do hope you could forgive me for being so petulant as to approach you unapproached, but we were wondering if it isn't too much trouble and you might consider it out of some sort of goodness of heart rather than anything else, if you think that it might be possible, seeing as you did originally say you would leave us here for eternity and it's been an eternity already, for you to consider willing to send us back.

Long stop

PHIL. No.

SISTER FATHER. Phil. I really need to talk to you.

PHIL ignores SISTER FATHER
All the other characters look at each other

THE SUICIDER. But you see...

HUSBAND. Yes, you see... we...

THE SUICIDER. We really want to get back.

PHIL. No!

SISTER FATHER. Phil, can I please talk to you!

THE SUICIDER. And we just thought that perhaps...

HUSBAND. Even if it were just for a day?

CHAIRMAN KESH. A day? No. I don't think that would be enough.

HUSBAND. Alright. Perhaps not a day.

DOCTOR HIIL. Just enough to quench our ambitions.

FATSO. Yes... we want to fulfil our wishes, Phil.

SISTER FATHER. Phil, can you please stop ignoring me.

BAKER. And if you let us live our lives.

SECOND WHORE. Yes... live our lives. That's right.

THE SUICIDER. Very short ones, mind.

HUSBAND. And just let us achieve our goals.

SISTER FATHER. Phil, I am asking you to please stop ignoring me.

HUSBAND. Perhaps let me love for a bit longer…

FATSO. Eat! I wouldn't mind eating a little bit more.

SISTER FATHER. It's very unpleasant for me.

CHAIRMAN KESH. I feel like I really deserve a bit more money right now…

DOCTOR HIIL. And I'm sure they're all going to need me down there…

SISTER FATHER. Phil, and I really need you to stop ignoring me.

SECOND WHORE. We wouldn't mind finding some more satisfaction.

FIRST WHORE. Finding it and giving it. We're not selfish, are we?

SECOND WHORE. Of course not.

THE SUICIDER. I would really like to be able to control my death, if you don't mind…

CAPTAIN KYIL. I want to save the world!

SISTER FATHER. Phil! Please stop ignoring me!

BAKER. And just to feed someone again. Just for a little short while.

CHAIRMAN KESH. Long while!

BAKER. Yes! Long while!

SISTER FATHER starts punching and kicking PHIL

SISTER FATHER. I asked you to stop ignoring me! I've had to sit here for eternity with these ruts and listen to them blaspheming. I've had to be here for eternity and have you, my one and only Phil ignore me. Ignore me for eternity. I will not take it any longer. You will now listen to me. You will listen to all of us. I've had it up to here. You will revive us all. You will open the door and let us all out. You will bring us back to the moment of our death and will ensure that we all achieve our goals. Is that clear?

All are stunned by SISTER FATHER's actions
As SISTER FATHER relaxes, PHIL manages to wriggle out, gets up, thinks for a moment and turns to the group

PHIL. Right. You all want to get back?

ALL. Yes.

PHIL. You all want to live your lives and achieve your goals?

ALL. Yes.

PHIL. Are you sure?

ALL. Yes.

PHIL. Right. I don't quite know what to say. I didn't really expect that from you. I guess I'm feeling slightly... overwhelmed. Slightly offended. Slightly... Slightly... Slightly... After taking such good care of you. After keeping you here for eternity, all you really want is to achieve these meaningless goals. And then maybe... for a while... I think... Perhaps... I don't know... Maybe... For a while. If nothing else, at least a while. All you would really rather do is go back to your menial meaningless lives. Moaning. Meaning. Mean. Mean. Mean... I mean... I am a mean man. Moan. Menial... Meaning lies... Meaningless... This is quite disappointing. Did we not have fun here? Did we not enjoy our eternity? I thought we had fun. I thought you enjoyed being with me. Now you all want to leave me. To live. To love. To leave to live and love. No! I just told you to not disturb me. You will all be quiet! I am sick and tired of this endless disappointment. Every time. Every single time. I do all I can. I do everything I can. I do everything. I do. I do. For you. For all of you. I do everything I can for all of you. And what do I get in return? Disappointment upon disappointment upon disappointment upon disappointment upon disappointment upon disappointment. One hundred disappointments... two hundred disappointments... four hundred disappointments... eight hundred disappointments... sixteen hundred disappointments... thirty two hundred disappointments... sixty four hundred disappointments... one hundred and twenty eight hundred disappointments... This is the truth. This is the right. This is the... You. All of you. In my head. You're all here in my head. You are all in my head. In my head. I asked you for something. Didn't I? I think I asked for something. I'm sure I asked for something. I always ask for something. There is always something to ask for. Always want something. Always wanting. Always wanting. Always doing. Always... always... and I... I... I... I am here. I am helping. I am making. I am creating... and I brought you all to life. And you came out of my head. Out of my mind. I must have been out of my mind. You're all out of my mind. Out of your minds! But mind your manners. You are not minding them today. I am hurt. I am not feeling nice. You are very impolite. Not nice. Not nice at all. You are not nice. You disturb. We are all disturbed. And I am in my mind. I am trying to... What am I trying? I am trying to do something. I am trying to get something. There is a point. There must be a point. You made this point. I made this point. I may disappoint. Point me to the nearest point. You are all to blame. Your fault. It's all your fault. You had great potential. You disappointed this point. That's it!

Long stop

I understand. Right. You all want to go back to life? Back to where I found you? As if eternity will be wiped away. And what is it that will be with me? Where will I end up? What will happen to me? If you all do what you wish. If you all do what you want. What will happen then? What will happen to me then. To me. Me? Me! What will happen... You will be down there, and I will sit up here. Like this. I will look down at you. Like This. I will be sad. Like this. I will cry. Like this. I can't stay here. I need to go. Where will you all go? A journey! There will be no journey. Who needs a journey? What's the point of going on a journey if you don't reach your destination? We need to get somewhere. You are here. You reached your goal. My goal. Our goal. A curse. A challenge. I guess... If... I mean… Only… If only… I guess… If I send you all back. If you all go back… I mean… I don't know. You confuse me. I think maybe you're right. I mean… perhaps we don't really have anything more to say. Nothing more to do. Nothing. Nothing. Not a thing. Nothing. No hope. No happiness. No hopiness. Yes. I mean… Yes. Perhaps we should. I guess I'll be lonely. If you all achieve your goals, what have I got left to do? Look at you? Look at you! Look at you with sadness. With disgust. No! This does not make any sense. None of this makes any sense. Substantial, sufficient, satisfying sense. I don't think that it can work. You will all be… Phil, what will they be? Phil! Philly? Silly Philly! What will they be? They will be! I can't be. I can't be here. I can't stay. I can't. Oh, my, I understand. You fulfil fully and Phil is futile. Phil won't feel or heal. Futile Phil! I have nothing more to do here! I'll join you!

Long Stop

I will send you back!

ALL. Thank you, Phil.

Scene 2 – Beginning Of The Road

The door marked 'Phil' opens, and from it enter the TWO WHORES and DOCTOR HIIL

FIRST WHORE. What a waste of our time.

SECOND WHORE. Nobody in.

FIRST WHORE. I'm sorry, Doctor Hiil for dragging you in here.

DOCTOR HIIL. It's quite alright. To be perfectly honest, I needed a little break.

SECOND WHORE. And did the break help you?

DOCTOR HIIL. Of course. It's not enough to heal the ill. The healed ill will die still so I must treat the dead. Not the sick! I have figured it out. I can create an immortalizing pill

FIRST WHORE. My shoe seems to be broken. Doctor Hiil, do you have a pill to heal my heel?

DOCTOR HIIL. No time for chitter-chatter!

DOCTOR HIIL exits

FIRST WHORE. Oh, Whore, look over there.

SECOND WHORE. What is it?

FIRST WHORE. Look!

SECOND WHORE. I'm looking!

FIRST WHORE. And you can't see them?

SECOND WHORE. Where?

FIRST WHORE. There!

SECOND WHORE. Oh…

FIRST WHORE. Can you see them?

SECOND WHORE. I can see them.

FIRST WHORE. Oh, Whore. I'm excited.

SECOND WHORE. Oh, Whore. I'm happy.

FIRST WHORE. They're here!

SECOND WHORE. They're finally here, Whore!

FIRST WHORE. And look…

SECOND WHORE. What?

FIRST WHORE. They're holding tickets.

SECOND WHORE. And a bottle of champagne.

FIRST WHORE. We are going to the theatre!

SECOND WHORE. Oh, look. They're wearing Tolstovka shirts.

FIRST WHORE. And Ushanka hats.

SECOND WHORE. I knew it! They are Russian!

Stop

BOTH. Caviar!

CHAIRMAN KESH enters through the door marked 'Phil'

FIRST WHORE. Oh, Whore, I must change my shoes. I can't meet them with a broken heel.

CHAIRMAN KESH. I can fix your shoes.

FIRST WHORE. Can you?

CHAIRMAN KESH. Yes… I can do anything I want to do for the right price.

SECOND WHORE. Oh, Chairman Kesh, We will pay you as much as you like.

CHAIRMAN KESH. You would?!

FIRST WHORE. We would.

CHAIRMAN KESH. I will take all your money, if I may.

SECOND WHORE. You may! You may!

They all exit as CAPTAIN KYIL enters

CAPTAIN KYIL. Well, there is nobody here. Excellent. The curfew worked. All the streets are empty and silent. All the people are tucked in their beds. All the justice is carried out and law is enforced. These are my streets and I am the only one allowed to be outside. How pleasing this is.

BAKER enters

Baker, what are you doing out here? The curfew, Baker. The curfew.

BAKER. Oh, I'm sorry, Captain Kyil. I can see, I can see it's past the curfew. I'll be straight on my way to the bakery. Would you like some muffins?

CAPTAIN KYIL. I would love some muffins!

BAKER. Really? Oh, Captain Kyil, that is the best news I've heard in eternity.

They exit as THE SUICIDER enters through the door marked 'Phil'

THE SUICIDER. I'm alive. I'm still alive. Oh, fate. Cruel fate to give me life when all I want is to take it away. How should I kill myself? What should I do? Guns failed... ropes failed... pills failed... acid failed... buildings failed... a train! That's it. I shall go and jump in front of a speeding train. I am all jittery and jumpy and tingly and pinny and needley and I am ready. How long till the next train passes? A quarter of an hour. Plenty of time to get there on time.

SISTER FATHER enters through the door marked 'Phil' – silent and forlorn

Oh, Sister Father, the train will pass in a quarter of an hour and I will ensure that my body will be laid on the track under its speeding wheels. Isn't that tingling?

SISTER FATHER is silent

Sister Father?

No response

Sister Fath… Oh, never mind. I must get to the tracks

THE SUICIDER exits
SISTER FATHER sits depressingly on the floor, where she had sat earlier in Act 1 Scene 5
PHIL enters through the door marked 'Phil'
SISTER FATHER is ecstatic

SISTER FATHER. Phil! You have arisen. My vow of silence brought you out! You have come out. Are you here for me? Who are you here for? What are you doing here? Why are you here? Is there a reason? Is it good, Phil? Is your presence here good? I can't believe you actually came out. You came for us. Will you stay? Are you stopping for long? Would you like a cup of tea? Would you like to sit here with me? I don't quite know what the etiquette is. I am not sure how I am to greet you. Oh, Phil. I can't believe you finally came. Please tell me you came for me.

PHIL. I came for you.

SISTER FATHER. Oh, Phil. That means… That means that I was right, doesn't it? And will you stay here with me, Phil? Will you?

PHIL. I will.

SISTER FATHER. Oh, Phil. You will? Did you hear that, everyone? Phil will! Phil will! Thank you Phil.

PHIL. You're welcome. Can I go now?

SISTER FATHER. Don't be silly, Philly. Come with me. You must come with me. Come and show everyone that you are real. My really, silly, Philly.

PHIL. Yes, Sister Father. Phil will. Phil will.

SISTER FATHER grabs PHIL violently by the hand and they both exit

Scene 3 – Home

WIFE stands over the cot

WIFE. Oh, my dearest child... we must ventilate the house. Of course we can cope without Husband. You and me, my dear child. That's all we really want. We don't need anyone else, do we?

(sings) You and me
You and me against the world
I could...
I could start working
I will find a job
And be supporting
Who needs a husband, eh?
I will be a single mum
I'll be a suffragette
I will be strong and independent
No, I'll be a modern woman
Who needs a husband, eh?
I could have it all
I'll have a career
I'll be a caring mum
I'll drink cocktails with my girlfriends

I'll be a mother
Yet a woman
A beautiful, sexy, successful and happy woman
I'll never miss your plays
I'll never miss your firsts
I'll never miss a date
I'll never miss a day's work
Never miss a thing
I'll have it all, I say!
Who needs a husband, eh?
I am a strong, independent woman
I am a mother, hear me roar!

WIFE roars loudly

Scene 4 – Bakery

BAKER, FATSO and HUSBAND stand in the bakery as they did in Act I Scene 4

BAKER. Eat. Food always solves conflicts.

FATSO. Fatso, this is your moment… Baker, Please give me as many cakes as you have. I will eat them all.

BAKER. Fatso, I'm thrilled to hear that. I have many new recipes I would like to try out on you.

FATSO. Thank you, Baker.

BAKER. But first, let me deal with Husband who's been waiting for quite a long time.

HUSBAND. I enjoyed watching your fraternity, though it did feel like an eternity.

BAKER. Heh… you sound like a poet.

HUSBAND. I realised that I spend my days searching for a love, and when it comes I give it a shove. I filled my life with new misery and brought my speech back to poetry. Oh Fatso, I need my wife. I want to rejoice in my old life.

FATSO. Well, you must go to her. Immediately.

HUSBAND. Yes. I will away. What a glorious day.

BAKER. And Husband, take some cake for your wife. Nothing says 'I'm sorry' like a piece of mille-feuille.

Wife enters the bakery

WIFE. Excuse me, Baker, I'm looking for a job, do you have…

HUSBAND. Wife! What are you doing?

WIFE. Husband! You're alive. I thought you were dead.

HUSBAND. No. It was a joke. A prank. I only meant to fool you and kid you and the kid into thinking that I was dead, but of course I'm not dead.

WIFE. Oh, Husband. I'm so glad that you're alive. I was so scared that you might be dead. A dead husband meant a dead end. And a dead end would have resulted in a deadly end for me. I couldn't speak. I couldn't walk. I couldn't breathe. Thank you for living. And to think I almost became a modern single mother. How dreadful! Thank you, Husband.

HUSBAND. What are you thanking me for?

WIFE. For your sense of humour. What a funny little prank that was. I think I am still giggling inside. Giggling like a giddy little girl.

HUSBAND. You are my giggly giddy little girl.

WIFE. I love you, Husband.

HUSBAND. I love you, Wife.

They are about to kiss…

WIFE. Oh, Child needs a feeding.

They exit the Bakery

FATSO. Now, Baker, feed me.

BAKER. Yes, Fatso.

FATSO. Fill me with your cakes.

BAKER. Yes, Fatso.

FATSO. Fill me with your breads.

BAKER. Yes, Fatso.

FATSO. Fill me with your éclairs.

BAKER. Yes, Fatso. Oh... Where do we start?

FATSO. I know. A doughnut. Baked with cheese and ham and drenched in chocolate sauce. With a cherry on the top and a cherry tomato on the bottom.

BAKER. Fatso, I will make it for you. And let's aim for it to end up just above your belly button.

Scene 5 – Monastery

HUSBAND and WIFE are standing full of joy

WIFE. Thank you for letting me grow this child together with you and making it the happiest child in the world. Together.

HUSBAND. Together.

WIFE. You and I.

HUSBAND. You and I.

WIFE. Happy?

HUSBAND. Happy!

WIFE. And in love.

HUSBAND. Of course. In love. Very much alive.

WIFE. And Child, we will both love you very much.

HUSBAND. For eternity?

WIFE. For eternity!

HUSBAND. I love how synched we are.

WIFE. We are in unison.

HUSBAND. In unison with the world.

TOGETHER. In unison with each other.

WIFE. In unison with our child.

HUSBAND. The three of us.

WIFE. And I can make this child…

HUSBAND. The most special being alive.

WIFE. Because our child is special.

HUSBAND. Most special.

WIFE. Like us.

HUSBAND. Just like us.

WIFE. Special and loving.

HUSBAND. Loving and special.

WIFE. Husband, it's as if…

HUSBAND. Our minds are like one…

WIFE. And we can complete…

HUSBAND. Each other's…

WIFE. Sentences…

HUSBAND. I…

WIFE. Love…

HUSBAND. You…

WIFE. So…

HUSBAND. Much.

They are about to kiss…

WIFE. Oh, Child needs…

HUSBAND. A feeding.

SISTER FATHER enters with PHIL on a leash

WIFE. Sister Father, it's magnificent.

SISTER FATHER. It most certainly is. Do you know who this is?

HUSBAND. It's Phil.

SISTER FATHER. Look! Phil's come. Phil's joined us. Phil's finally with us. And look. Phil, speak!

PHIL. Hello!

SISTER FATHER. Isn't it a dream? Just like I've always imagined it.

HUSBAND and WIFE exit

Phil. Tell me another story.

PHIL. Legend tells of a pointless being, who wandered around the world aimlessly. The being was saddened by the lack of meaning in it all and didn't want to waste time on emotions, so decided to concentrate on doing. Another pointless being was also wandering around the world aimlessly. That being didn't mind the lack of meaning in it all but also didn't want to waste time on emotions, and decided to concentrate on being. The being that concentrated on the being and the being that concentrated on the doing met one day and decided to wander around the world aimlessly together, and not waste time on emotions together…

PHIL is disturbed by the entrance of CHAIRMAN KESH

CHAIRMAN KESH. Sister Father, I've come to collect your money.

SISTER FATHER. Oh, yes, Chairman Kesh. I won't be needing it ever again. Look who is here with me.

CHAIRMAN KESH. Oh… is that Phil?

SISTER FATHER. It is! It is!

CHAIRMAN KESH. Hello, Phil.

SISTER FATHER. Shake hands, Phil.

PHIL shakes hands with CHAIRMAN KESH

CHAIRMAN KESH. Phil is adorable.

SISTER FATHER. That's what I thought.

CHAIRMAN KESH. So… money?

SISTER FATHER. Oh, yes. Of course.

SISTER FATHER gives CHAIRMAN KESH a lot of notes

Come on, Phil. We must go and see more people. Show them the truth has finally arrived.

SISTER FATHER leaves with PHIL
CHAIRMAN KESH starts counting the notes

CHAIRMAN KESH. Ten… Twenty… Thirty… This is amazing! Forty… Fifty… Sixty… Incredible. Seventy… Eighty… Ninety… Unexpected! One hundred… One hundred and ten… One hundred and twenty. This is beyond my wildest dreams.

CAPTAIN KYIL enters

Captain Kyil, I need your money.

CAPTAIN KYIL. Right away, Chairman Kesh.

CAPTAIN KYIL gives CHAIRMAN KESH more notes

CHAIRMAN KESH. Thank you so much. More money for me.

CAPTAIN KYIL. But Chairman Kesh. You're outside past the curfew. I must shoot you now.

CAPTAIN KYIL shoots CHAIRMAN KESH who falls dead

Another outlaw. Another body.

CAPTAIN KYIL exits
DOCTOR HIIL enters from the other side

DOCTOR HIIL. I heard a gun shot. Who's dead? Oh, poor Chairman Kesh. Here, I will fix you.

DOCTOR HIIL attends to CHAIRMAN KESH who wakes up

CHAIRMAN KESH. Doctor Hiil. How nice to see you. I will take all your money now.

DOCTOR HIIL. Of course, Chairman Kesh.

DOCTOR HIIL gives CHAIRMAN KESH more notes
CHAIRMAN KESH starts counting them
BAKER runs in holding bread rolls
FATSO follows, eating

BAKER. Doctor Hiil. A terrible thing happened. The Suicider drowned!

DOCTOR HIIL. I'm on it!

DOCTOR HIIL runs out
BAKER approaches CHAIRMAN KESH

BAKER. Chairman Kesh, I have some bread for you.

CHAIRMAN KESH. I will sell you my stomach.

BAKER. Thank you, Chairman Kesh. Here is all my money.

BAKER gives CHAIRMAN KESH more notes in exchange for some bread
CHAIRMAN KESH counts the notes and exits gleefully

I have more bread! Who wants more bread?

TWO WHORES enter

SECOND WHORE. Oh, Baker. We will take your bread. We need it for our caviar.

BAKER. Wonderful.

BAKER gives the WHORES the bread and exits
FATSO finishes eating and follows

FATSO. Baker, I'm finished! I need more!

FIRST WHORE. It's the interval.

SECOND WHORE. What a play!

FIRST WHORE. What a play!

SECOND WHORE. Such twists.

FIRST WHORE. I did not expect to see that.

SECOND WHORE. I rooted for the characters, and then it just came out of nowhere.

FIRST WHORE. It was so unexpected.

SECOND WHORE. And the songs?

FIRST WHORE. Oh… beautiful!

SECOND WHORE. Moving!

FIRST WHORE. What more do you want from theatre?

SECOND WHORE. Real and genuine emotions.

FIRST WHORE. Yes. I really connected emotionally. Didn't you?

SECOND WHORE. Oh, yes. isn't that what art is all about?

FIRST WHORE. And the acting?

SECOND WHORE. Superb!

FIRST WHORE. Such magnificent acting.

SECOND WHORE. Believable!

FIRST WHORE. It was almost like peeping into their lives.

SECOND WHORE. I thought it was a documentary.

FIRST WHORE. Such skill.

SECOND WHORE. Such beauty.

FIRST WHORE. And the caviar?

SECOND WHORE. Sublime.

FIRST WHORE. Whore?

SECOND WHORE. Yes, Whore?

FIRST WHORE. I'm running out of superlatives to describe this evening.

SECOND WHORE. I know.

FIRST WHORE. Too perfect.

SECOND WHORE. Too perfect.

FIRST WHORE. And our friends…

SECOND WHORE. They were Russian alright.

FIRST WHORE. We call them Kalinka and Babushka.

SECOND WHORE. Such good people.

FIRST WHORE. Such good souls.

SECOND WHORE. Whore, are you satisfied?

FIRST WHORE. I am.

SECOND WHORE. Me too.

FIRST WHORE. We must get back.

SECOND WHORE. Before they notice we disappeared.

FIRST WHORE. We don't want to miss the second act.

SECOND WHORE. Oh yes. I heard that in the second act everything is reversed.

Scene 6 – Town Centre

THE SUICIDER lays motionless centre-stage
BAKER and FATSO sit upstage. BAKER is feeding FATSO. Both look tired
After several seconds of repetitive feeding, DOCTOR HIIL enters
Characters seem jaded and almost robotic, as would be expected after doing the same thing over and over again for a long period of time

DOCTOR HIIL. What happened?

BAKER. The Suicider again.

DOCTOR HIIL. What happened this time?

BAKER. Jumped off the building.

DOCTOR HIIL. Oh, dear.

DOCTOR HIIL attends to THE SUICIDER who wakes up

THE SUICIDER. Oh, Doctor Hiil, you saved me.

DOCTOR HIIL. Yes. I saved you.

THE SUICIDER. Thank you.

DOCTOR HIIL. You're welcome.

THE SUICIDER. Right. How will I kill myself now? What day is it today? Is it Monday already? Well, I haven't suffocated myself for a long time, have I?

DOCTOR HIIL. No. I do believe not since last Thursday.

THE SUICIDER. Well, suffocation it is.

DOCTOR HIIL. Alright… Let's go.

DOCTOR HIIL and THE SUICIDER exit

BAKER. How is this one, Fatso?

FATSO. Same as before. Delicious.

BAKER. That's nice. Any new fat?

FATSO. I believe above my knee there is a new lump.

BAKER. That's lovely. Right. We are out of profiteroles. What would you like to eat now?

FATSO. Shall we move on to pitta breads?

BAKER. Oh yes. Pitta breads. Come.

FATSO. Where are we going?

BAKER. To the bakery. I have a special exotic section where all my pitta breads are placed.

FATSO. Come on.

Before they manage to get up, CAPTAIN KYIL enters, shoots them both dead and exits
After a few moments HUSBAND and WIFE enter
WIFE is holding the child
They are both talking in an almost robotic state

HUSBAND. Oh, Wife. My beautiful, loving wife.

WIFE. Yes, my dear Husband.

HUSBAND. Bodies.

WIFE. Yes, husband. Poor bodies.

HUSBAND. Oh, my ray of sunshine. I think we should call Doctor Hiil.

WIFE. Oh, my munchkin honey pot of joyful sweetness. Let's call Doctor Hiil.

TOGETHER. Doctor Hiil!

WIFE. Again, we are…

HUSBAND. In perfect unison.

WIFE. That makes…

HUSBAND. Me happy.

WIFE. Yes, completely…

HUSBAND. And utterly…

WIFE. Ecstatic.

HUSBAND. Kiss me.

WIFE. Child needs a feeding.

WIFE exits with HUSBAND running after her
DOCTOR HIIL enters and without saying a word attends to FATSO and BAKER.
They wake up and DOCTOR HIIL exits

BAKER. To the bakery?

FATSO. Yes, let's get the pitta breads.

FATSO and BAKER start exiting
SISTER FATHER enters with PHIL on a leash

SISTER FATHER. Look, Fatso. Look, Baker, it's Phil.

FATSO. Yes, we know, Sister Father.

BAKER. You've shown us several times.

SISTER FATHER. But look! It's Phil. Phil is real! And I was right!

FATSO and BAKER exit
SISTER FATHER sits on PHIL

Oh, Phil. Tell me a new story.

PHIL. I'm out of stories, Sister Father.

SISTER FATHER. Oh… But what do we do now?

PHIL. Nothing.

CHAIRMAN KESH enters with notes sticking out of every pocket – speaking in an excited yet somewhat monotonous manner

CHAIRMAN KESH. Look at all my money! Look at all my money!

SISTER FATHER. Chairman Kesh, look! Phil!

CHAIRMAN KESH. I know! Look! Money!

CHAIRMAN KESH exits as the WHORES enter

SISTER FATHER. What do you mean, nothing? How can we do nothing?

FIRST WHORE. Another play, Whore?

SECOND WHORE. Another play!

FIRST WHORE. Some more caviar?

SECOND WHORE. Some more caviar!

FIRST WHORE. A sip of champagne?

SECOND WHORE. I love champagne.

CAPTAIN KYIL enters, shoots the WHORES and exits

PHIL. I mean nothing.

SISTER FATHER. But you're here.

PHIL. I am. We're together. Isn't that enough?

SISTER FATHER. You're right. It's enough. I'm happy.

DOCTOR HIIL enters, attends to the WHORES who wake up, and exits

SECOND WHORE. Another play, Whore?

FIRST WHORE. Another play!

SECOND WHORE. Some more caviar?

FIRST WHORE. Some more caviar!

SECOND WHORE. A sip of champagne?

FIRST WHORE. I love champagne.

As lights start to fade, we see the following actions repeating in a loop:

1. BAKER and FATSO enter. BAKER is feeding FATSO, running behind. They pet PHIL on the way

2. THE WHORES enter and lean on the wall

3. CAPTAIN KYIL enters and shoots them all. They all fall dead

4. DOCTOR HIIL enters and attends to all four, who wake up and exit

5. CHAIRMAN KESH enters counting money and exits

6. HUSBAND and WIFE enter holding hands. They are about to kiss and WIFE runs away, HUSBAND follows

7. THE SUICIDER enters with a gun/plastic bag/pills and commits suicide

8. DOCTOR HIIL comes and attends to THE SUICIDER who wakes up and they both exit

BLACKOUT

Fulfill Me Fully, Phil - Opening

Lyrics: Sebastian Rex
Music: Noam Galperin

17
D Am7 D9
me, I have no wife My
19
B B7/D♯ E
name is Doc-tor Hiil I'm here if you feel
22
C♯ø F♯ A♯m/F A♯ø D♯7
ill and I am Cap - tain Kyil pro-tec-ting
25
G♯ø C♯m7 F♯7 B A♯7
you in the name of Phil If
28
E♭M7 D♭/E♭ A♭/E♭
you are in a cri - sis and need a com-for - ting
31
E♭ G7/D C C7/B♭ F/A Fm/A♭
ear this is Sis - ter Fat - her she's

34
C/G G B♭7 E♭M7
real - ly quite a dear If a - ny-one is
37
D♭/E♭ A♭/E♭ A♭m/E♭ E♭ D 7(♯5)
hun-gry the bake-ry's o - ver there but the
40
G m C m7 F 7
cakes are too de - li-cious so you bet-ter all be -
43
B♭ B♭7/D
ware We live a per - fect life we're
46
E♭ C F 7 F 7/E♭
hap - py as can be so please en-joy our
49
D 7 G 7sus4 C 13 F 13(♭9)
town and come to vi - sit

B♭ B♭7/A♭ E♭/G E♭m/G♭ B♭/F C7/E
52
me and me and me and me and me and
E♭m B♭/D B♭m6/D♭ C7 BM7 F7 B♭7
55
me and me and me and me no, me
E♭M7 D♭/E♭ A♭/E♭
58
3
I'm the hap-pi-est per-son I'm hap-pier than
E♭ G7/D C C7/B♭ F/A Fm/A♭
61
him I'm hap-pi-er than both of them to-ge-ther
C/G G7(♭9) B♭7(♭9) E♭M7
64
I'm ac-tual-ly quite grim We're al-ways all so
D♭/E♭ A♭/E♭ A♭m/E♭ E♭ D7(♯5)
67
hap-py and that's all thanks to Phil we've been

70
Gm
Cm7
A7/C♯
hap - py since cre - a - tion and we're
72
D9
G9
C9(b13)
F7(♭9)
B♭
B♭7/A♭
hap - py e - ver still We're
75
E♭/G
E♭m/G♭
B♭/F
C7/E
hap-py hap-py hap py hap-py hap py hap-py hap-py hap-py
77
E♭m
B♭/D
B♭m6/D♭
C7
hap py hap-py hap py hap-py hap py hap-py hap py hap-py
79
B M7
F7
hap py hap - py hap py hap - py

Cravings

Lyrics: Sebastian Rex
Music: Noam Galperin

17
D♭
A♭9(♯5)
For - ty kinds of choco - late with sar -
19
B♭m7
F 7(♯5)
F♯7
dines on the side
Mar-mite fon -
22
B m7
E 7
A 7
duc and a swan that just died
25
D(add9)
F♯7/C♯
B 7(♭9)
Piz - za with bread-crumbs and ap - ri-cot
28
E m7
F M7
C (add9)
cheese and final - ly a milk - shake from
31
D 7
G 7
spi - nach and peas

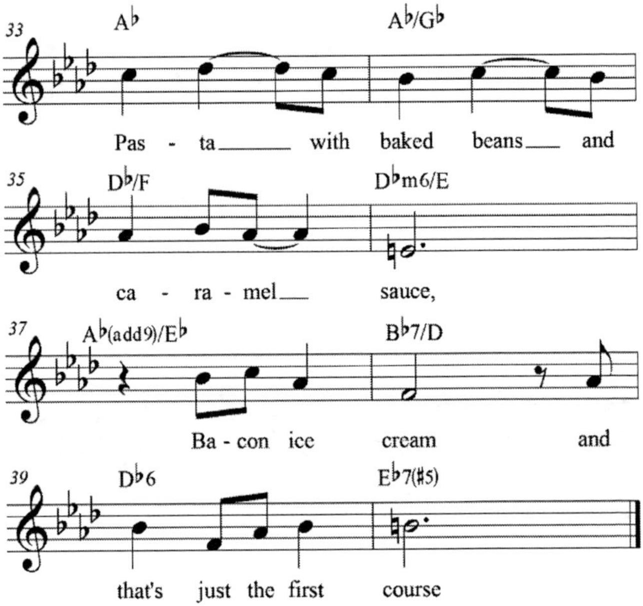
33
A♭
A♭/G♭
Pas - ta___ with baked beans___ and
35
D♭/F
D♭m6/E
ca - ra - mel___ sauce,
37
A♭(add9)/E♭
B♭7/D
Ba - con ice cream and
39
D♭6
E♭7(♯5)
that's just the first course

My Dearest Child

Lyrics: Sebastian Rex
Music: Noam Galperin

Noam Galperin - 2011

My Dearest Child

F♯/A♯ F♯m/A A♭7 D♭sus4 D♭7
that you, so young she has to smo - ther.
F♯m E B/D♯ D A
Yes, dear - est child I'm feel - ing un-well,
F♯7 Gm Dm D7
my men - tal world is cons - tant hell.
E 7(♭5) A 7(♭9) A♭M7(♭5)
I'd ra - ther die and burn for e - ter - ni - ty
F♯7(♭9) A♭7(♯5) A M7(♭5) B 7 B 7(♯5)
than live with you post this ma - ter - ni - ty.
Em C/E A/E F♯7(♭9) B7
My dear - est child your fa - ther waits,

Who Needs a Husband, eh?

Lyrics: Sebastian Rex
Music: Noam Galperin

Cm/E♭ A♭9 F7 B♭7♭9♯5
suf - fra-gette I will be strong and in - de -
E♭ D♭7(♯11) C7(♯5)
pen - dent No, I'll be a mo - dern wo - man
Fm9 G7♭9♯5 C7(♭9)
Who needs a hus - band, eh? I could
F(add9) F♯°7
have it all I'll have a ca - reer I'll be a
Gm9 B♭°7 C7
car - ing mum I'll drink cock - tails with my
Fm9 D♭7 G7(♭9)
girl - friends I'll be a mo - ther Yet a

23
Cm7 B
wo - man A beau - ti - ful, se - xy, suc -
25
E♭/B♭ A° A♭m6 G7♯5♭9
cess-ful and hap - py wo - man I'll
28
Cm9 A♭M7(♭5) D° Fm7
ne-ver miss your plays I'll ne-ver miss your firsts I'll
30
E♭M7 A♭9 F7 B♭7♯5♭9
ne-ver miss a date I'll ne-ver miss a day's work
32
E♭sus4 E♭ D♭7(♯11) C7(♯5)
Ne-ver miss a thing I'll have it all, I say!
34
Fm9 G7♯5♭9 C7(♭9)
Who needs a hus - band, eh?

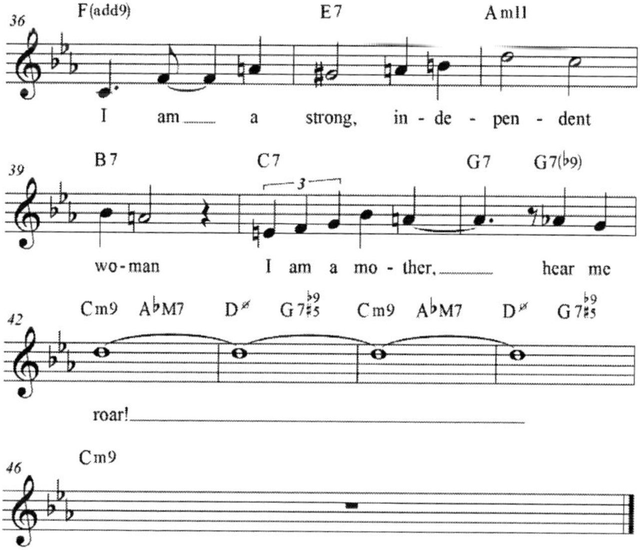
36
F(add9) E7 Am11
I am a strong, in - de - pen - dent
39
B7 C7 G7 G7(♭9)
3
wo-man I am a mo - ther, hear me
42
Cm9 A♭M7 D⌀ G7♭9♯5 Cm9 A♭M7 D⌀ G7♭9♯5
roar!
46
Cm9

Playing With…

These two plays are performed in one evening with the same cast:

Toby / Harry
Thomas / O
Charlie / Veronica
Ann / Maddy
Bernie / Ingrid

Playing With... was first performed at The Blue Elephant Theatre, London under the name *"Toy Boy and Living With... - A Sebastian Rex Double Bill"* Between 11-29 of November 2008 with the following cast:

Toby / Harry	Ben Kettner
Richard / O	Ido Gonen
Charlie / Veronica	Emma-Rachel Blackman
Ann / Maddy	Elizabeth Pinnock
Bernie / Ingrid	Elena Rossi
Thomas	Tom Radford
Alisa	Stacey Lamb

Living With…

Characters (In order of appearance):

Ingrid
O
Harry
Veronica
Maddy

O and Ingrid enter a small room with a single bed, a chair and a small table. A big chest is situated on the table at the back of the room. O is wearing black trousers and a white t-shirt and carries a big backpack. Ingrid is wearing a dress.

INGRID. And this is the bedroom.

O. It's nice. Very nice. It looks perfect.

INGRID. Well, as you can see there's only a single bed here and the heating doesn't always work, but it's alright, really.

O. It's great. I love it. If you guys are happy with me moving here, I'll take it.

INGRID. We should be able to give you an answer now. Just give me a minute.

O. That's great.

Ingrid leaves the room and closes the door slowly.
O looks at the room. He sits on the bed and tries the mattress. It is very soft and seems like it's been used by many people.
After a few moments Harry opens the door and sticks his head in. he stares at O. O is conscious of him looking at him but doesn't look back. Eventually he looks up. Harry forces a big smile and leaves, closing the door gently.

O. Stay positive. Things can't get any worse.

Veronica enters the room.

VERONICA. OK... Wait!

Veronica rushes out and leaves the door open. Harry comes back and closes it gently.

O. OK...

After a few moments the door opens slowly. The three of them come in.

INGRID. If you want the room, it's yours.

VERONICA. We'd be happy to have you here.

INGRID. You seem like a really nice guy.

HARRY. And attractive...

INGRID. And you can stay here with us.

HARRY. We'd love to have you here.

VERONICA. We'd love it.

INGRID. Love.

O. When can I move in?

HARRY. As soon as you like. The place is free.

VERONICA. It's yours now.

INGRID. We'll have a party tonight.

VERONICA. You drink, right? It will be fun.

HARRY. We'll give you some time to settle in and sort out your stuff.

INGRID. We'll see you in a few minutes.

O. Oh, OK…

Ingrid, Harry and Veronica leave the room and shut the door violently.
O takes a moment and starts to unpack his bag. He takes out 3 sets of black trousers and white t-shirts and puts them on the bed.

I told you. A bit of positivity will not kill you. We're here now and everything is going to be fine. We'll be fine. From now on our life will only get better and better. A party… a party… I'm not sure I'm in the mood to party. Come on, new flatmates. They look like fun. You can socialise. I know you can. It will be great. Alcohol. A lot of alcohol. What more do you need? What should I wear?

The final item in his bag is a big scarf. O takes it out and looks at it.

Don't! Don't! Everything is going to be OK. Everything is OK.

He hides the scarf under the bed as the door opens. Harry enters.

HARRY. Hey, finally, a male flatmate. Fabulous. I tell you what, it can get a bit tiresome to live only with girls. But there are some good things about it too, if you know what I mean. You do know what I mean, right? Well, girls... you know... when they come out of the shower. Wait, I didn't mean to assume. You do like girls, don't you? You know what? Don't tell me. Let me find out for myself in due time. I don't care either way. Whatever makes you happy. As long as you like sex, I don't give a fuck who you do it with. You do like sex. I mean, you look like a good boy, but seriously, who doesn't like sex? And Veronica and Ingrid are... Phowar. I tell you what, you have moved into the right house. Living with me will be the best thing that's ever happened to you. You and I are going to have...

Veronica enters holding a bottle of spirit and wearing a dress.

HARRY. *(Whispers to O)* When she gets out of the shower, it sometimes falls off, you know?

VERONICA. Here, have a drink. Ingrid will be here in a minute and then we can get this party started. Do you drink? Oh wait, I've already asked you. I'm sorry. I sometimes forget things. Drink.

Veronica hands him the bottle.

O. What is this?

VERONICA. A… a drink.

O. Do you have a glass?

VERONICA. Fuck the glass. Who needs glasses?

He is about to start drinking from the bottle.

WAIT! You can't drink like that. You have to make a toast first, you idiot.

O. Oh, OK… Well, here's to flatmates.

VERONICA. Bollocks! Here's to hopes and dreams. May you never have any.

O. Huh?

VERONICA. Now drink!

O drinks.

O. What the hell is that?

VERONICA. I told you! A drink! You don't like it?

O. No, it's good. It's just strong

VERONICA. Of course it's strong. It's a drink.

Harry whispers something in her ear.

Ahhhh, I'm sorry. I should have explained myself better. This is an alcoholic drink

O. Yes, I know that.

VERONICA. Good. So drink more.

O drinks more.

That's enough. My turn again. I must tell you, it's great having you around here. Finally I can have someone to look at. Harry isn't the handsomest of people, Ahh, who am I kidding?! He's an ugly piece of shit.

HARRY. Fuck you!

Harry pushes Veronica violently. She crashes onto the wall.
O is shocked but they both start laughing.

Ingrid enters wearing a short tight dress and smoking a cigar.

VERONICA. What are you smoking?

INGRID. It's just a cigar, darling.

O. Aren't you cold?

HARRY. Ingrid's never cold. Do you know why I know that? Because her nipples never stick out.

INGRID. *(Laughing)* Shut up, you pervert. *(To O)* Do you smoke, honey?

VERONICA. Why would anybody smoke honey? You're so stupid sometimes.

O. Yes, I do. Socially.

INGRID. Do you want one?

Ingrid gives him a cigar and lights it for him seductively.
O is mesmerised but as he is about to actually light it, the doorbell rings and Ingrid jumps.

INGRID. Shit!

Ingrid runs out.

O. Is everything alright?

HARRY. Of course. Why shouldn't it be?

O. I…

VERONICA. You want another drink!

O. Oh, I…

VERONICA. I knew it. You don't like it.

O. No, I do like it, but… I'm still digesting the first one

VERONICA. That's not very nice of you to not like my drink. Come on. Have a drinky-poo.

O. I…

VERONICA. Drinky-drinky!

O. But…

VERONICA. It will make a man out of you. It will grow some hair on your chest.

HARRY. You don't have hair on your chest?

VERONICA. Come on! Drink!

HARRY. You better drink it. She can go on for a very long time.

O takes the bottle.
He starts to drink.

VERONICA. STOP! I hope you're not retarded or something. I told you. You have to make a toast. What do you want this one to be for?

O. How about happiness...

VERONICA. Yeah. May you never know the meaning of the word.

Ingrid enters the room with a big cake.

INGRID. Cake.

VERONICA. Drink.

INGRID. Do you want a slice?

VERONICA. Drink, damn it.

INGRID. I made it just for you.

VERONICA. Drink! You bloody arsehole.

Silence.

After a moment Harry, Ingrid and Veronica start to laugh. O looks confused. They eventually calm down and the room turns silent again.
They stare at him, and after a few seconds of uncomfortable silence -

O. Who lived here before me?

INGRID. I don't actually remember. Some guy.

HARRY. It was a girl.

VERONICA. No, it wasn't. It was a guy.

HARRY. I'd remember if it was a guy. It was a girl.

O. Where did she move to?

VERONICA. He… and I don't know.

INGRID. So many people lived in this room, it's hard to remember.

O. Oh, really? You've had many flatmates?

INGRID. A few… I'm sorry. I forgot to give you a cigar…

O. How many people lived here before me?

HARRY. Did we give you your key?

O. No.

INGRID. I forgot.

HARRY. I'll go get it.

Harry leaves.

INGRID. So where did you live before? You seemed to be stressed for a place.

O. Yes, I had to move out urgently…

INGRID. Well?

O. Well what?

Harry enters the room.

HARRY. Here it is. Now listen, about the key. We ask you only for one thing. If you ever manage to move out of here, please make sure to put the key in this chest. That's the only thing that's important for us.

O. That's not a problem.

The doorbell rings. Harry runs out.

INGRID. Don't let her in!

O. Who is that?

VERONICA. We're good flatmates. We're very nice to live with... How were your last flatmates?

O. You know...

INGRID. No, we don't actually.

O. It's not important.

Harry enters.

HARRY. Sure it is. Hey, in this house there are no secrets. Now tell us. Who did you live with?

O. It was all very messy and I'd rather not talk about it.

INGRID. Oh, don't be like that. We never keep secrets here.

VERONICA. You can't hide anything from us.

INGRID. We find out eventually. You'll see.

HARRY. It's true. Ingrid's amazing. She is like a telepath or something. Try her. Think of a number.

INGRID. No, don't do that.

HARRY. Come on. Think of a number. You'll see. Ingrid will guess it.

INGRID. Harry, don't do that to the poor boy.

HARRY. He's not poor and he's not a boy. He'll love it. Come on. Sit down. *(O looks hesitant)* I said sit down.

O sits on the chair.

Now think of a number. You're not thinking. Are you thinking?

INGRID. Leave him alone.

HARRY. Shut up. *(To O)* Look at me. Look me in the eyes. I want to see if you're thinking. You're not thinking. Are you thinking? Think. Think! I want to see you think. You're not thinking of anything.

O. I have a number.

HARRY. Don't just have a number. I want you to think about it. Think long and hard about that number. Don't stick it in your mind like a dog. Think about it. Contemplate on it. Its shape. Its meaning. Its being. I want to see the essence of the number on your skin. I want to see it flowing through your veins. Your mind is not fucking working!

He grabs his throat.

Think, idiot!

Veronica grabs Harry and pushes him on to the bed.

VERONICA. Get off him, you animal.

INGRID. I'm sorry about that. He's just a wanker.

VERONICA. *(To Harry)* Here, drink some more. *(To O)* Are you OK? He didn't hurt your pretty face?

O. No, I'm fine. Don't worry about it.

HARRY. I'm sorry.

Silence.

INGRID. 30 million.

HARRY. What?

INGRID. The number.

HARRY. Was that correct?

The doorbell rings. Veronica leaves the room.

INGRID. If you don't want to tell us about your last flat, you don't have to.

HARRY. Maybe we should all go to bed.

INGRID. Bed? No! We're having a party. You don't have to tell us anything now if you don't want to. Have some cake. Smoke a cigar. Let's all relax and have fun.

Veronica enters the room. The other two exchange glances with her.

O. That sounds good to me. Can I have another drink, please?

Veronica hands him the bottle.

VERONICA. Don't finish it.

O. And I'll have a piece of that cake please and a cigar.

Ingrid gives him a cigar.

VERONICA. It's finished.

HARRY. What is?

VERONICA. The alcohol.

HARRY. Go get some more.

VERONICA. No. You get some more.

HARRY. You drank it all.

VERONICA. So what?

HARRY. So you should go.

VERONICA. You drank some of it too.

INGRID. Why don't you both go? We'll stay here and eat some cake like civilised people.

VERONICA. Who are you calling uncivilised. I'll have you know that I come from a very posh family. My grandfather owned a country in Africa. I can eat with a knife and fork if I want to, and I can walk and talk like a lady if I want to, and I can say polite words like 'pardon' if I want to, and I can wear corsets if I want to...

HARRY. You do wear corsets.

VERONICA. I do. I do. That's right. Where was I?

HARRY. Corsets...

VERONICA. Yeah. And I can play cribbage and croquet if I want to, and I can buy servants if I want to, and I can play the flute if I want to. Thing is... I don't want to. I want another drink. Harry, come with me. I might even show you my knickers if you do.

HARRY. You don't have to bribe me. I'd come anyway. I think Ingrid wants some time alone with him.

They leave.

INGRID. That's right. We're going to eat cake. Do you like cake?

O. Do you know what, I actually really do.

INGRID. Eat.

Ingrid hands him a slice.

Do you want me to feed you?

O. OK.

INGRID. You promise not to bite?

O. Sure.

The doorbell rings again.

Who is ringing the doorbell all the time?

Ingrid starts to feed him small pieces.

As she speaks, she gradually starts feeding him bigger pieces and quicker until it reaches the point where he doesn't manage to swallow.
As this happens, Ingrid becomes more and more forceful.

INGRID. You know, this is a very nice flat. But some of the neighbours are a little bit crazy. We just need to ignore them. We can do whatever we want here. It's only us three, well, us four here. You'll love it. And I have a good feeling about you. You're a nice guy. A good guy. But can I ask you a question? I'm surprised you're here. You know, most of the people we get here are horrible. Really horrible. I hated most of our flatmates, but you… you're adorable. I can't understand why you would have to settle for a shit hole like this. Heh. This room is disgusting and filthy. I don't know why anyone would want to come and live here, but we always manage to find a tenant. I don't know if people are stupid or desperate… What are you? Stupid or desperate? I don't care. As long as someone pays the rent, I'm happy. We've had a few terrible flatmates. I was glad when they left. But you'll stay, right? I hope you'll stay. No one ever stays…

O starts choking.
He spits the cake out.

I'm sorry. I got carried away. Are you OK? I'm so sorry…

O. It's fine.

INGRID. I'm sorry. I ruined the cake.

O. The cake was lovely. That was the problem. It was too good. I couldn't say no.

INGRID. I am so sorry for doing this to you.

O. Look. It's not your fault. I enjoyed it. I could have closed my mouth.

INGRID. You're lovely.

Veronica and Harry enter with 4 bottles.

HARRY. Are you doing it yet? Look what we brought. More booze.

VERONICA. Do you know what they are?

O. Drinks?

VERONICA. Exactly.

HARRY. What the hell happened here? Did you have sex?

INGRID. We had cakes.

HARRY. Did he tell you why he fucked up his last flat?

O. I didn't fuck anything up.

HARRY. Hey, if you want to be secretive about your past, it's our prerogative to make up whatever truth we see fit.

VERONICA. So until you tell us otherwise, you fucked it up, and you're a disgusting failure.

INGRID. Veronica!

VERONICA. But a sexy failure.

HARRY. These are all your clothes?

O. Yes.

HARRY. That's all you brought?

O. Yes.

HARRY. A man of few belongings and fewer words. I think we can have a lot of fun with you. Can I try your clothes on?

O. Can I have a drink?

HARRY. Of course you can. You don't need to ask.

O. Well, I do need the bottle.

Harry gives him the bottle.

Here's to… a lifetime of misery.

VERONICA. He's got the drift. You're not retarded after all. A lifetime of misery!

HARRY. A lifetime of misery. Great. Now can I try your clothes on?

O. Of course you can. You don't need to ask.

Harry undresses and puts one of O's sets of clothes.

VERONICA. Are you digesting it better now?

O. It's the best drink I've ever had.

VERONICA. Really? Do you mean it?

O. It's delicious.

INGRID. How was the cake?

O. Also delicious.

VERONICA. But the drink was better, right?

O. They were both delicious.

INGRID. No. You have to choose one. What was more delicious? The cake? Or the drink?

HARRY. I'll tell you what's delicious. Me. In these clothes.

INGRID. You look ridiculous.

HARRY. Shut up. Let's see how you look in them.

He grabs Ingrid, undresses her and puts another one of the sets on her. Though he is very violent, she keeps laughing.

VERONICA. I feel all left out. Come, you friends, undress me now.

HARRY. *(Still busy with Ingrid)* Do you want to take care of that?

O. Sure. Why not.

O starts to undress Veronica gently.
She struggles and slaps him hard.
He starts being more forceful until he manages to control her and undress her. He then puts a set of his clothes on her.

HARRY. Look at us. We all match. We are delicious!

VERONICA. I'm bored. Let's play a game.

HARRY. *(Pushes Veronica away)* Girls. This is time for some gender-bonding. You play with yourselves.

VERONICA. No. We'll have one more drink together. One bottle each. Let's see who finishes the bottle first.

They each hold a bottle and stand in a circle.

Are you all ready? We'll drink to never ending agony.

HARRY. A life time of sickness!

INGRID. Constant ugliness!

O. And to an inevitable death!

VERONICA. 1… 2… 3… go!

They start drinking.
They force themselves to finish the bottle and every once in a while one of them wretches.

I win. Fuck you all!

Veronica breaks her bottle on O who collapses onto the bed.
She falls on top of him.

HARRY. Yeah!

Harry jumps on top of them.

INGRID. Stop it!

Ingrid pulls Veronica and Harry off of O who is bleeding.

Shit. You're bleeding. Are you OK?

Harry falls next to the bed and picks up the scarf.

HARRY. What's this?

INGRID. Give me that.

Ingrid takes the scarf and puts it on O's head to stop the bleeding.

Relax. Everything's going to be OK. Have a cigar.

Ingrid is about to give him a cigar as O begins to cry. Veronica and Harry, who are still trying to catch their breath, are staring at him.
Ingrid cradles him like a baby and tries to soothe him. Meanwhile she lights a cigar and sticks it in his mouth.

O. *(Coughs and wretches)* Just leave me alone. All of you. I'm OK. Let me go.

Ingrid keeps holding him, and the cigar still stuck in his mouth.

Let me go. I can't breathe.

Ingrid holds him even stronger.

Let me go. Let me…

O pushes out of her grip and falls on the chest.
It bursts open and hundreds of keys fall out.
The doorbell rings.
Ingrid exits.
O takes a moment looking at all the keys.

O. How many people lived here before me?

Harry takes the scarf and sits in front of O.
He places it on top of O's face, covering his eyes and his mouth and pulls back forcefully.
Offstage we hear Maddy shouting and slapping Ingrid.

MADDY. *(O/S)* Let me in now!

Maddy enters. She's wearing a dress and a black jacket over it.
Ingrid comes in after her holding her face in pain.

MADDY. What's going on here?

Harry gets off O and throws the scarf at him.

(To O) Are you alright?

HARRY. Maddy, everything is fine. You can go.

MADDY. I heard noises. Is everything OK?

INGRID. Of course it is. Why shouldn't it be?

VERONICA. We're having a party.

MADDY. *(To O)* You're bleeding. And you're shivering.

Maddy gives him her jacket.

HARRY. We're just having a bit of fun...

VERONICA. Yeah. Just some fun.

INGRID. Fun.

MADDY. But he's hurt.

INGRID. I know he's hurt. I was taking care of him.

MADDY. *(To O)* Have you been drinking?

VERONICA. He only drank a little bit.

HARRY. Maddy, we were playing with each other. You know the score.

MADDY. Why aren't you talking?

O doesn't respond.
Maddy shakes him gently.

Are you alright? Say something.

O still doesn't respond.
Maddy slaps him hard on his face.
O cries and cradles into Maddy's arms.

MADDY. What did you do to him?

INGRID. We…

HARRY. We had…

VERONICA. We had a party.

MADDY. *(To O)* Don't worry. I'm here now. I'll take care of you…

Maddy leaves O, who is lying on the floor playing with his scarf.

You think this is fun? Look at him. He's sick and miserable. How can you do this to him?

INGRID. We just…

MADDY. I know what you just. You just gave him cake. And cigars. Give me your cigars.

Ingrid seems tentative.

Give them to me!

Ingrid gives Maddy the cigars.
Maddy crumbles the cigars and sticks the tobacco in Ingrid's mouth. She then grabs Ingrid by her hair and pushes her face into the cake.
Ingrid falls on the floor crying.

VERONICA. Hey… Don't do that.

Maddy pushes Veronica and she collapses on the wall.
Maddy takes one of the bottles and empties it on Veronica.
Harry begins to laugh.
Maddy notices what he's wearing.

MADDY. Why are you all wearing the same clothes? Are these his? *(To O)* Are these yours?

HARRY. We wanted to see if they fit us.

MADDY. Take them off!

Harry stares at her.
Maddy grabs him by his crotch and pushes him to the chair.

Take them off! Go on! *(To Veronica and Ingrid)* All of you.

Veronica and Ingrid begin to undress.
Harry growls under Maddy's grip and she releases him so that he could take his clothes off.
While they all undress, Maddy collects their other clothes and throws them out of the room.
The three stand in a straight line wearing nothing but underwear and looking down.

I think the party's over.

The three begin to leave the room.

VERONICA. Remember, if you're moving out, put the key in the chest.

Veronica exits.

HARRY. Key in the chest.

Harry exits.

INGRID. Key. Chest.

Ingrid starts to leave but then she comes back, kisses O and whispers in his ear.

I hope you stay.

Ingrid exits and the door bangs.
Maddy looks at the mess in the room.
She then notices O has tied the scarf around his neck to look like a noose.

MADDY. What's the matter with you? What are you doing?

O gets up, with his scarf still tied as a noose and sits on the bed.

O. I've had enough.

MADDY. Don't be stupid...

O. But I am stupid. I'm a stupid stupid person. I've been stupid from the day I ruined everything. And now I pay.

Maddy comes behind him and grabs the scarf, it seems as if she's about to release it but she grabs it and carries O on the floor choking him.
O is lying on the floor. Maddy sits on his stomach and grabs his hands.

MADDY. Get up!

O struggles to get up. Maddy forces him to the floor.

Come on, you stupid person. Get up!

O starts to cry.

Don't cry. You're pathetic! Get up! Come on!

O. I don't want to be here any more. I want everything to be back the way it was… I want my old flat.

MADDY. So why don't you go there?

O. I can't. I've handed in my notice. I had to leave. They found a new flatmate now. I wasn't thinking properly. I knew better and I knew right and I knew wrong and I knew all these things, and now all I have is this place, and I don't want to stay here. This place is a dump. Look at it. Who'd want to live in a room like this? It's horrible. The flat is cold, and I'm all alone here and they are horrible people and I'm in pain. So much pain. And I don't like it here and I don't want to be here anymore. I just want my old life again.

Maddy instantly becomes very maternal, gets off O and starts to cradle him.
At some point she gets up with him and they start to dance. At first they dance slowly, but gradually it becomes more manic.

MADDY. What are you talking about? You're wrong! This flat is great. Yes, the people living here are a bit… But I live next door and I can come every day and be with you and play with you and help you and have fun with you.

You poor poor thing. Look at me! Stop thinking! Think about nothing. Just look at me and forget everything. You have nowhere to go. Nowhere at all. Stuck here with these three monsters. Don't worry. Maddy is here now and she will take good care of you.

O. Really?

MADDY. Of course. I'm here for you.

O. Help me.

MADDY. Of course I'll help you.

O is so dizzy he collapses on the bed.

I will come every day.

O. What?

MADDY. New rules! New rules! Let's make a list! I love lists!

O. Yes.

MADDY. I will come every day. At 6pm!

O. Yes.

MADDY. We will have a lot of fun together, and we will never invite the others to join us.

O. Yes.

MADDY. And if I hit you, it's because I care about you.

Maddy slaps O strongly. O begins to cry.

Oh, baby.

Maddy cradles him.

And you must kiss me whenever I tell you to.

Maddy starts kissing O on his face until they eventually kiss.
The kiss gradually becomes violent.
Maddy eventually pushes O off and gets up.

MADDY. If you do as I tell you, I will control these maniacs and keep them out of your life.

Maddy slaps him and they both giggle.

O. Thank you so much.

MADDY. You don't need to thank me. Go to sleep. Tomorrow everything will be much better.

O. Will you come again?

MADDY. I will come every day.

O. Thank you.

MADDY. At 6pm.

O. Yes.

MADDY. You do want me?

O. Yes.

MADDY. Are you sure?

O. I'm positive.

THE END

Toy Boy

Characters:

Toby
Thomas – late 20's
Ann – mid 20's
Charlie – early 20's
Bernie – late 30's

The play takes place in different locations and over one year.

Scene One

(Kitchen. Toby is sitting alone on a chair. Throughout the whole scene, Voices are heard offstage indicating there is a party going on in the other room)

VOICES. Ten... Nine... Eight... Seven... Six... Five... Four... Three... Two... One... Happy New Year!

TOBY. *(To himself)* There is nothing to fear; this will be a happy new year...

BERNIE. *(Enters from the living room)* Toby, m'darling, there you are. Brilliant party, there are so many people here. I was looking all over for you. I wanted to kiss you at midnight... I love those countdowns. Two... One... Happy New Year. *(She kisses him and takes his party hat off)* You're awful quiet tonight. It's alright. You know me. I like my men with a mouthful. OK, I'm off, I'll call you tomorrow. *(She starts to exit)*

TOBY. I shall walk you to the door. Though if you stay, I won't be sad anymore.

BERNIE. What was that? *(She puts lipstick on)*

TOBY. *(He gets up, they start walking towards stage left)* It doesn't matter what I said. I can come with you to your bed.

BERNIE. Oh, babes, that's so cute... No. I'm going to another party. *(They exit. As they leave Bernie shouts into the room)* Happy New Year.

(Charlie storms in from the living room and exits into the bathroom. Thomas comes in after her)

THOMAS. Look, I'm sorry, alright? It's difficult to apologise when you're locked in the toilet. Don't be stupid! Come out, now! I'm sorry! Really! I'm Sorry! I'm Sorry! I'm Sorry! I'm Sorry! I'm Sorry! I'm Sorry! I'm Sorry! I'm Sorry! I'm Sorry! I'm Sorry!

ANN. Excuse me... Thomas, is it?

THOMAS. Not now! *(To Charlie)* Come out or I'll start singing... OK. I'm going to do it. I'm going to sing. *(Pause)* Ann, say something!

CHARLIE. *(Off)* My name isn't Ann!

THOMAS. Fuck!

CHARLIE. *(Off)* My name isn't fuck either!

ANN. *(To Thomas)* I'm Ann! She's Charlie!

THOMAS. What do you want?

ANN. When I came to the party, you said, "How are you?" and I said "Fine!" I lied… well, not lied, I was just wrong. The truth is I have a bit of a cold. Oh, don't worry… nothing serious. I don't think there are many chances of it being contagious, I mean… you're not going to catch anything just by talking to me. We're only talking! It's not like we're kissing or anything. I mean… not that I want to kiss you. I wouldn't dare dream of that. No! I wouldn't mind kissing you, but I… I don't… You won't catch it. The flu… You won't catch the flu! From me! *(Pause. Toby enters and sits unnoticed)* Oooh… I like your hat.

THOMAS. And my hat likes you! *(To Charlie)* Come out! Now!

ANN. *(Goes to the bathroom door)* Charlie, what's wrong? Are you alright?

CHARLIE. *(Off)* Yeah, I'm fine.

ANN. No, really… Are you sure you're alright? You can tell me.

CHARLIE. *(Off)* Yes! I am!

ANN. Can I come in? Do you want me to come in? Can I come in?

CHARLIE. *(Off)* No! I told you I'm fine!

ANN. OK, but you *are* sure?

CHARLIE. *(Off)* Yes! Now fuck off, Ann!

ANN. Oh dear… *(Looks at all the other people, embarrassed)* OK…

TOBY. Don't worry, she'll be alright. I don't think she was very polite. You really are a very good friend, and I have no doubt she'll apologise in the end.

ANN. *(Sees Toby sitting)* Hi, who are you?

TOBY. My name is Toby, madam, how do you do?

ANN. I'm not sure madam is appropriate, but thank you. I'm Ann. *(Charlie comes out of the toilet)* That's it, Charlie! You really have crossed the line. Now, listen to me, this time I know exactly what I want to tell you. You are pathetic and you are…

CHARLIE. Shut up!

THOMAS. Dear God, the two of you are freaks.

ANN. I beg your pardon.

THOMAS. Beg, bitch!

ANN. *(To Charlie)* Shall we go?

CHARLIE. No. I want to stay a bit longer....

THOMAS. Hmmm...

ANN. What?

THOMAS. Nothing... Just hmmm...

ANN. Well, I'm leaving. Happy New Year.

TOBY. Happy New Year, my dear!
May there be no fear,
And may your goals be clear
And may your eyes never...

THOMAS. AAAAH! *(He slaps Toby. Charlie and Ann look confused)*

Scene Two

(Ann and Charlie's living room. Charlie and Thomas enter)

ANN. Oooh... I didn't know you stayed the night.

CHARLIE. Yeah, we're going out. *(Looks in her bag)* I forgot my toothbrush.

THOMAS. Hurry up. *(She exits)*

ANN. It was a good party.

THOMAS. I don't remember much of it, though.

ANN. Oh dear, I'm Ann.

THOMAS. Yeah, I remember you. You were pestering Toby.

ANN. Toby… yes. I was talking to him… I hope he didn't get too drunk.

THOMAS. I doubt it.

ANN. Well, say hello to him from me, if he remembers me.

THOMAS. Toby doesn't do relationships.

ANN. What? What's that got to do with…?

THOMAS. Stop asking me questions! That's the way he is. He does whatever I tell him to do. He's a good boy and right now he's dating Bernie.

ANN. Bernie?

THOMAS. She was at the party.

ANN. But… but… if he doesn't like it, why does he do it?

THOMAS. Look. I'm only telling you what he's like! *(Shouts offstage)* Charlie, are you coming?

ANN. Where did you meet him?

THOMAS. I found him somewhere, bought him, got him at an auction... What does it matter? *(Shouts offstage)* Charlie!

CHARLIE. *(Off)* Shut up!

ANN. I don't think I like the way you talk about him.

THOMAS. He's Toby. *(Giggles. Charlie enters)*

CHARLIE. Come on. *(They start leaving)*

THOMAS. If you want something from him, let me know and I'll arrange it. *(They exit)*

ANN. No! I want to understand!

Scene Three

(Bernie and Toby enter the stage dressed as bride and groom. Toby has his eyes closed)

BERNIE. Oh Toby... I would like to declare my undying love for you.

TOBY. *(Opens his eyes and comes towards Bernie)* Oh, Bernadette, it's great to be here alone, just us two.

BERNIE. Come with me, my horse is outside. Let us go and till eternity ride. I want to be with you forever and a day, Oh, soon, we will be so merry and gay…

TOBY. Oh, it's nice… oh, it's great! That I finally found a mate… Someone who could hold me strong, whisper love words so I belong.

Scene Four

(Bernie's bed)

TOBY. I didn't expect you to say that at all, but then again, it is your call. Do you want to think about it one more day, this might not be the only way. Is there really no chance that this relationship will ever advance? Bernadette, tell me, is it something I've done? I thought we had some good times. Did you have none?

BERNIE. Got a fag? *(He shakes his head)* Crap! I've lost my lighter… Why are you still here? Didn't I just break up with you? Got a lighter? *(He shakes his head)* Why are you still here? Wait! You're a good shag, aren't you? *(He doesn't respond)* Well, are you? Never mind, Go!

Scene Five

(A bar. Charlie is sitting facing the audience.)

CHARLIE. So how do you find me? *(Pause)* Come on, you can do better than that. You have wonderful muscled arms. You work out? *(Pause)* Do you find me sexy? *(Pause)* Yes, from one to ten. Go on. What would you rate me as? *(Pause)* Once again, I think you can do better than that. *(Pause)* Don't you dare touch me. *(Pause. She shouts)* All I wanted was a drink! Wanker. *(She composes herself and turns to face another direction)* Right. Hello there. You're a model, right? *(Pause)* Really? Looking at you, I just assumed. So what do you do? *(Pause)* Wow, how fascinating. I've always been interested in that. *(Pause)* I'm waiting for someone. I wouldn't dream of sitting here by myself all night. My breasts are far too beautiful. It would be selfish not to show them. *(Pause)* You're silly. Of course you can't touch them. *(Pause)* How dare you! I suggest you leave now before I throw my drink at you. *(Pause. She sighs and slumps down)* Tom! Come back.

THOMAS. Why did you stop? It looked like it was going so well.

CHARLIE. It got boring. Come on, I can't do this cheerful slut thing. Anyway, what were you doing back there? Were you just getting off on looking at me?

THOMAS. Hey, mind your own perversions.

CHARLIE. *(Toby enters)* Toby, what are you doing here?

TOBY. *(Towards Thomas)* Thomas told me to come here. He made that clear.

CHARLIE. Really? We're on a date.

THOMAS. Toby, don't you want to give me a hug? *(Whispers in his ears)* Make her jealous. *(They hug for a long time)*

CHARLIE. What the hell are you doing?

THOMAS. You know, good friends.

CHARLIE. Toby, go away. *(Toby exits)* You are so mean to him.

THOMAS. Mean? What are you talking about? I love that creature to bits.

CHARLIE. Love?! Oh, and Ann wants to date him too..

THOMAS. That's fine. Bernie's finished with him, so he's free. But isn't making him go out with Ann cruel?

CHARLIE. You're horrible. You know what, I'm going home.

THOMAS. What? I thought you might like to talk.

CHARLIE. What do you want to talk about?

THOMAS. Nice weather, eh?

CHARLIE. I'm not going to sit and talk about the bloody weather.

THOMAS. OK. Sorry... I'm just trying to be romantic.

CHARLIE. I thought you don't do romance.

THOMAS. I'm serious. *(She smiles at him. He kisses her)* Hmmm...

CHARLIE. What?

THOMAS. Nothing... Just hmmm... *(They kiss again, but he abruptly stops her)* Goodnight! *(Leaves)*

CHARLIE. That's it? Hit and run?

Scene Six

(Restaurant)

ANN. So eventually, my boss came in and started shouting... at *me*. And she sat there, said nothing and let me take all the blame. Now my boss wants to talk to me on Monday.

TOBY. Ann, you seem very stressed. I'm sorry that you're feeling depressed.

ANN. It's not your fault. Why do you keep apologising for things that have nothing to do with you?

TOBY. I'm sympathising... it's just something I do.

ANN. Rejoice with them that do rejoice and weep with them that weep. *(Pause. He stares at her)* That's from the bible. I hope you don't mind me quoting from it.

TOBY. I don't know where it's from, I must admit.
ANN. You don't know what the bible is? *(He shakes his head)* really? I'm... it's a beautiful book. You must read it. I can't believe you never heard of it. *(Pause. She looks at him, full of sincerity)* What's your story? *(He looks at her bewildered)* Oh, come on... you must have one.

TOBY. I have none.

ANN. I can see in your eyes that something has happened to you.

TOBY. *(Panics)* That's not true.

ANN. Toby, what's wrong?

TOBY. Let's go somewhere else, not for long.

ANN. Do you want to go somewhere else? *(He nods)* OK... let's go. Is there a nice pub anywhere near?

TOBY. Unless of course you want to stay here.

ANN. No! You want to go somewhere else. You have a right to decide what we do…

TOBY. No! It's all up to you!

ANN. *(Shouts)* Stop it! Sorry I shouted at you! I didn't mean to offend you.

TOBY. I'm alright. I'm having a really nice night.

ANN. So shall we go to the pub or for a walk…

TOBY. Perfect, a walk! And then we could talk. End the night in the middle of a park, with the moon above, sitting in the dark. Perhaps a kiss, to end the night, but only if you think it's right.

ANN. Charming…

Scene Seven

(Lights change. All the characters sit around a table. Toby lies on it with his eyes closed)

BERNIE. I told him how amazing he was…

THOMAS. And let me guess, he believed you. *(She nods)* Told you he has no flaws. We have created the perfect creature, and have you tried his best feature?

CHARLIE. Try saying something like 'I love *you*'... For you it's a lie, for him it's a cue.

BERNIE. This thing will be a hit in the shops. We can manufacture him with added props.

THOMAS. Ann, you're seeing him now, right? Try using these key words on him, tonight.

ANN. I think he's sweet...
(Pause. They all look at her. She notices she said something wrong , panics, and struggles to find a rhyme) I mean, to eat! *(They laugh)*

TOBY. *(Gets up)* I don't want to die, I just want to cry! *(He repeats this as a mantra)*

Scene Eight

(We cut to the Kitchen. Charlie and Thomas)

THOMAS. You want a drink?

CHARLIE. Yes!

THOMAS. What drink?

CHARLIE. I said yes!

THOMAS. Yes what?

CHARLIE. Yes! I want a drink!

THOMAS. *(Yells)* What do you want to drink?

CHARLIE. Don't yell at me!

THOMAS. I'm sorry. I'll get you a drink!

CHARLIE Orange juice.

THOMAS. Fine. I'll get Toby to get you some.

CHARLIE. I'm sick of that game! Are you addicted to him or something?

THOMAS. What's your problem with Toby?

CHARLIE. He's boring.

THOMAS. Look. You just need to learn how to play with him. That's it. Tell you what. You sit here. I'm going to call him in and leave you to it. Pet, stop watching cartoons and go give Charlie a massage.

(Thomas leaves. A few moments later, Toby enters and starts giving Charlie a massage)

CHARLIE. Toby, do you like me? Do you think I'm attractive? No, don't answer. I know your answer is going to be yes, and if it isn't, you probably didn't understand the question. Do you think Tom likes me?

TOBY. Thomas loves you, that's very true. We all love you. I love you too.

CHARLIE. Of course you love me. You love everybody, everybody loves you, I love you too. *(Pause)* Come on, pet, kiss me!

(They kiss, Thomas enters)

THOMAS. Hmmm…

CHARLIE. What?

THOMAS. Nothing… Just hmmm… *(Charlie storms off)* Toby, listen, I want to ask Charlie to marry me. Don't look so surprised. I'm getting to a certain age… Stop looking at me like that. I need to get married. *(Toby shrugs)* And I love Charlie. I wouldn't marry her if I didn't love her. Thing is, I'm scared she'd say no, and then I'd have to dump her and I really don't feel like confrontation. So I want you to be there. Anyway, don't think I don't love you anymore, because I do! And don't worry. I still want you to be with us and play with us and help us and have fun with us… coz you're my little pet, right? *(Toby blushes* *and nods)* You'll always be my best little friend. *(There's a knock on the door)* Go to your room!

BERNIE. Hello, babes, you alright?

THOMAS. Yes.

BERNIE. I'm not too bad, love, not too bad at all.

THOMAS. You broke up with Toby. why do you still keep coming here?

BERNIE. Actually, that's why I'm here. Came to speak to Toby, didn't I.

THOMAS. What for?

BERNIE. It's none of your business... I need to talk to him about what happened to me last night.

THOMAS. What do you want to tell him?

BERNIE. It's personal.

THOMAS. Come on Bernie, I know you. Just tell me what happened to you.

BERNIE. What you on about? It's personal, innit?! Very personal!

THOMAS. Fine!

BERNIE. Well if you must know, a few nights ago I went out with some friends, just down to the local, it was a karaoke night. Anyway, there we was, singing our little hearts out, pissed as hell! Oh, I was singing Tom Jones' "Delilah", in case you was wondering. My friend Audrey was telling me that a nice suited gentleman dragged himself in and sat down by the bar. So, anyway, I went over to the bar and I saw this bloody Adonis. I'm not lying to you. He was a bloody Adonis. Well, I'm sure you know what I'm talking about. Can you imagine the perfect guy? Better. Anyway, he had this whole dark mysterious look about him… oooh… sent shivers down my spine. So there I was, using all me flirty tricks to try and get him to buy me a drink, and he did… obviously! And we was talking… Well, actually, I did all the talking. The guy didn't say a single word the whole evening. That bastard didn't even ask me for my name. So I was talking to him and all of a sudden it was last orders and I was all tipsy-like so I said "Where you off to now?" and he still didn't say a word. He just got up, and started walking out. So I said "mind the company?" and he shook his head. Anyway, to make a long story short, we was in his car on the way to his house, and he was still saying nothing. I was babbling my brains out, talking about anything and everything… What are you giving me that look for? Oh come on… you know I'm not that kind of girl. He seemed nice.

THOMAS. Nice? The bloke didn't say a single word.

BERNIE. He did! Eventually…

THOMAS. After you shagged him.

BERNIE. Fuck off! I didn't shag him!

THOMAS. Come off it, Bernie, what do you want?

BERNIE. I want Toby. I need to talk to him.

THOMAS. Yeah, well… Toby's busy.

BERNIE. Tom… I didn't sleep with that guy…

THOMAS. Wasn't big enough for you?

BERNIE. How dare you! You want to know what happened? We was just snogging and I didn't want to go any further, so he grabbed my hair and opened his mouth for the first time. Do you know what he said? "You like pain, bitch?" The only sentence I heard from him all night.

THOMAS. Did he rape you?

BERNIE. No! I hit him back. I gave him a black eye and a few bruises, actually.

THOMAS. So what do you need Toby for?

BERNIE. I need to know that people don't just want me for a shag… and that my personality is also nice.

THOMAS. *(Gets up)* Is it?

BERNIE. *(Serious, all of a sudden)* I don't need this right now, Tom.

THOMAS. *(He starts leading Bernie to the door)* He's watching cartoons at the moment…

BERNIE. Thomas, I need Toby now! Give him to me now!

THOMAS. *(He opens the door)* I'll tell him you was looking for him, innit. *(He closes the door)*

Scene Nine

(Dark room. Toby sits alone)

TOBY. I feel tears in my throat and a pinch in my heart, I feel like my whole world is falling apart. There's only one thing I ask from above. The one thing I'm missing is someone to love…

I don't want to die, I just want to cry!

THOMAS. Toby, stay here. Oh, and Bernie wants you to come over for dinner to make her feel that she's good for more than just sex. Good luck.

Scene Ten

(Lights change. Thomas opens the door to Bernie and Charlie)

THOMAS. Guys, it's Toby's birthday today.

BERNIE. Yes! Let's do something special, OK?

CHARLIE. Let's throw him a surprise party, and get lots of stuff!

THOMAS. Cakes and chocolates... but that's not enough!

BERNIE. Why don't we cook him a gigantic meal?

THOMAS. And get him a heart so he could love and feel! A lovely red heart in a multi-size pack.

CHARLIE. And then he could finally love us all back.

(They approach Toby who is still with his eyes closed)

BERNIE. Toby, it's your birthday...

THOMAS. Toby, come with us!

TOBY. I know it is my birthday, but there's no need to fuss.

BERNIE. We're off to see the wizard to get you a pink heart, come and hold my hand, so that we'll never part!

(Toby gets up. He stands to Bernie's right and puts his arm in her arm. Thomas stands on Bernie's other side, and Charlie on Toby's other side)

THOMAS. To the wizard we go...

CHARLIE. To his magical dome!

TOBY. There's no place like home! There's no place like home! *(Repeated)*

Scene Eleven

(Bernie's flat)

BERNIE. ...Toby!

TOBY. I'm ever so sorry I was miles away... Tell me again, what did you say?

BERNIE. No, forget it, go home! I don't want you to stay the night! If you do, you might get dirty thoughts. And I'm not going to shag you tonight!

TOBY. I don't like you just because you look so great, I like you because you cook and can hold a serious debate. Dinner was a real delight, I shall go now, so good night!

BERNIE. You know what? You can stay!

TOBY. Bernadette, you're very beautiful but you know, you're not that kind of girl so I must go!

BERNIE. Toby, I changed my mind!

TOBY. You told me not to stay, so I best go away!

BERNIE. Go to hell, Toby! *(Throws him out and slams the door after him)* I'm so ugly!

Scene Twelve

(Kitchen. Charlie enters)

THOMAS. Good. You're here. Toby and I wanted to talk to you about something. I'll get him.

CHARLIE. Why is he always here?

THOMAS. What do you mean? He lives here!

CHARLIE. So he just happened to come into the kitchen without you calling him?

THOMAS. What are you talking about?

CHARLIE. Why are you always with him?

THOMAS. He makes me happy.

CHARLIE. Well. I'm here to make you happy now, and he is just annoying.

THOMAS. Charlie, What do you want from me?

CHARLIE. I never get a minute alone with you!

THOMAS. Hmmm...

CHARLIE. What?

THOMAS. Nothing! Just hmmm...

CHARLIE. Why are you always humming? *(Thomas starts laughing)* What the hell are you laughing at? *(He laughs harder)* Thomas! Thomas! I'm sick of this! Call me when you grow up. *(She starts to exit)* And don't call me! *(She exits)*

THOMAS. Crazy bitch! Toby! *(Toby enters)* What's wrong with her? I never know when she's joking and when she isn't. Do you think I'm making a mistake? I mean, I like her. She's OK... I mean, I love her. But then she gets all like... I don't know. I want a hassle-free life. Perhaps marriage isn't the best option for me. Saying that, I am getting old... well, older! What if I never find anyone else? I know, that's stupid. Of course I will. But getting married can be nice. I could have a big party, get loads of presents, go on honeymoon, do the sex, live blissfully for a couple of years, and then in the worst case, get a divorce. It's just a new experience I've never had. And I think it could be a lot of fun. Everybody gets married. It's like going to Australia! I need to learn more things. Experience more things. If I want to be a better person, I should learn more and more and experience stuff, shouldn't I? Yeah, I think it will be good to marry her, live with her for a few years and divorce her.

Scene Thirteen

(Ann and Charlie's living room. Toby knocks on the door. Ann opens. He enters with flowers and chocolates)

ANN. Toby, what are you doing here? Are these for me? *(He shakes his head)* I was planning on coming to visit you. I wanted to give you something. I happened to see it in a shop so I bought it... I hope you like it! *(She gives him a wrapped present. He tries to open it very slowly)* Just open it. I want you to see what it is. *(He opens it and takes out a bible)* Look, it's a bible! *(Toby looks bedazzled)* If you don't like it, I'll take it back.

TOBY. No! Don't take it away. I just don't know what to say.

ANN. Don't worry... It's not going to make you religious or anything like that, but this book has so many stories to tell, you can just read it on and on and on... and on... so I bought it because I thought maybe we could read it together. You know, a little bit every day.

TOBY. Why does religion scare you so much? Or is this a topic you'd rather not touch?

ANN. Oh, my father... He is a very religious man, and... He believes, because he's uhm... religious. Look, this is *really* not important. *(She looks at him)* You don't like it, do you?

TOBY. *(Eagerly)* No! I really do! But I want to listen to you. I would much rather you talked about your father.

ANN. No, it's OK.... Look, I have to go!

TOBY. No!

ANN. Toby... I really have to go! I'll see you tomorrow at the party, OK?

TOBY. Ann, please don't go away! *(He grabs her as Charlie enters)*

CHARLIE. What are you doing here?

TOBY. I got you some flowers and some chocolates too, just to show you that Thomas really loves you.

CHARLIE. What the hell...? Where's Tom?

TOBY. Thomas couldn't come today. He asked me to visit because it was on my way! He sent me to give you these things, and a kiss. But if you don't want it, you can give it a miss.

CHARLIE. A kiss? You are such an idiot! Get away from me! You are nothing! Just a foul disgusting creature! *(Pause)* You know, Toby, I don't get you! What's your problem anyway? Don't you understand that they're all using you? Why are you doing this to yourself? How can you live knowing that nobody really loves you? Oh, yeah, I forgot. If someone loves you, you won't be able to cope with it. *(Toby doesn't move)* Just go away!

TOBY. Fine, I will go away, but before I do I have one thing to say! Even though I don't know why you say I have no life, I was asked to ask you *(Kneels down on his knees in front of her)* Will you be Thomas's wife?

CHARLIE. Now listen to me! Stay away from me! Stay away from Tom! Get yourself a life and stop ruining ours!

TOBY. I'm sorry Charlie! *(He starts to leave the room, and mumbles as he is exiting)* Hope you enjoy the chocolates and the flowers!

ANN. You are horrible.

CHARLIE. For fuck's sake! Just tell him you love him and get it over with.

Scene Fourteen

(Toby is sitting at home reading the bible. All of a sudden he gets up and closes his eyes)

TOBY. Honey, I'm home, I missed you today. *(Ann enters, Toby opens his eyes and is delighted to see Ann)*

ANN. Honey… at last! I was waiting all day. Toby Junior is mowing the lawn and look at this picture Tobina has drawn *(She shows him an empty piece of paper)*

TOBY. Oh, that's so great. Our kids are so swell.

ANN. Oh, yes, I know. We brought them up well.

TOBY. *(Yells)* Kids, come on in! Your daddy is here! *(To Ann)* What are we having for dinner my dear?

ANN. It's Manna bread! Our family's favourite food.

TOBY. Manna bread?! Oh, honey, Life is so good!

Scene Fifteen

(Toby goes to open the door. Ann and Charlie enter)

ANN. Happy New Year. I missed you.

TOBY. So did I, my dear. I was so excited about seeing you, I couldn't think clear.

THOMAS. Charlie! What are you doing here?

CHARLIE. I need to talk to you. I thought about what you asked me.

THOMAS. Shall we go to my room? *(They exit)*

ANN. Toby, would you like a drink? *(She goes to the fridge)* I need to tell you something. It's very strange for me to talk about this. Do you remember when I was telling you about my father? Well… there was a reason why I didn't want to talk about it. The thing is, he was very religious and his moral standards were… he was very strict. He had strong beliefs about what is good and what is evil. He believed that everything was corrupt and he didn't want us to be affected by the disgusting sacrilegious world out there, so he kept us at home and didn't let us leave the house. We were home-schooled. We only went out for church, and even there we couldn't talk to anyone… One day when I was eight, I was sitting in the garden, and a newspaper page flew in from over the fence. It had a comic strip on one side and a weather forecast on the other. It looked so pretty. I took it inside and showed it to my mother. She started crying and said, "Get rid of this immediately! Don't let your father catch you with that filth!" I meant to throw the paper away, but I couldn't do it. It had names of places on it, and names of people and funny little pictures. It looked so strange and interesting, so I kept it inside my dolls' house. Well, it was a big brown box. I called it a dolls' house because my rag-doll lived there. I don't remember where I got her from. I think I always had her. I played with her so much. My father wouldn't let me have any other toys apart from her. I think my mother forced him to let me keep her. So I would play with her and talk to her and share my secrets with her, and I hid the piece of newspaper with her. I used to look at it every night before I went to bed and read bits of it to my doll. Then one night, I guess I was reading it a bit too loudly and my father burst into the room. I quickly hid it under the covers. He came towards me and looked me straight in the eyes, I couldn't look back at him. I was shaking so I lowered my face, but he leaned forward, grabbed my head and lifted it so I had to look into his eyes. He asked me "What are you doing?" and I said "Nothing, Father! Going to bed!" He came closer and threw away my covers. He picked up the paper and said: "What is this?" and the only words that came out of my mouth were "*She* found it" and I pointed at my doll. He looked at me and then at the doll and he grabbed her and said: "Well then… she must be punished for bringing that kind of filth into my house and corrupting my little girl". He turned away and said "Come with me". He pulled me out of bed and into the garden. I was only wearing my nightie and my feet got all muddy and my father said: "All sinners must be punished by God". He took a box of matches out of his pocket, lit one of them and set fire to the paper. It went in such big flames. He dropped it on the ground, put the doll in the middle of the fire, lit another match, threw it on her, then he lit another match and another one and another till she was all burnt. He kept on saying: "All sinners must be punished by God... All sinners must be punished by God" and all I could think of is that I loved my doll, but I blamed her and she burned because of me. I've not really wanted to love anything ever since. But Toby, you have changed my life so much... You talk so sweetly and make me smile! You showed me that I am worthy of much more than I thought and... Toby... I love you!

TOBY. You actually mean it, you do?!

ANN. Yes, I do...

TOBY. Ann... I love you too! *(They kiss)*

THOMAS. *(Enters the room with Charlie)* Sorry to disturb. Toby, Come in! Charlie and I want to talk to you.

TOBY. Not now!

THOMAS. What?

TOBY. I said not now... I can't come now because I'm busy! Just leave me alone! *(Charlie enters)* All of you! Come on, Ann, let's go!

THOMAS. Go where? Toby, what's wrong?

TOBY. Get away from us! We want to be alone!

CHARLIE. Tom, he's not rhyming.

TOBY. Just leave us alone! I don't want you to bother me now! I... I... I... I... I... I... I am talking to Ann now, and... and... and... and... and... and... that's more important to me than your stupid problems! So leave us alone now, and... and... and... and... and... let us talk. The word of the Lord came to me saying: go and proclaim in the hearing of Jerusalem, Thus says the lord:...

CHARLIE. What the hell is he saying?

ANN. That's from Jeremiah.

TOBY. ... I remember the devotion of your youth, your love as a bride How you followed me in the wilderness, in a land not sown... So I'm sick of you all always wanting me to do stupid things. And I'm sick of you needing me for every little thing that you do. And now I want to be alone. Leave me alone. His wife Jezebel came to him and said, "Why are you so depressed that you will not eat?" He said to her, "Because I spoke to Naboth the Jezreelite and said to him, 'Give me your vineyard for money; or else, if you prefer, I will give you another vineyard for it'"...

THOMAS. Toby, that's enough!

ANN. Toby, stop! Please! Let's go away.

CHARLIE. Ann, what's wrong? Are you alright? No, really… Are you sure you're alright? You can tell me.

TOBY. …But he answered, "I will not give you my vineyard." His wife Jezebel said to him, "Do you now govern Israel? Get up, eat some food, and be cheerful; I will give you the vineyard of Naboth the Jezreelite"… I love Ann and Ann loves me and we are going to be happy, and… and… and… and… I think you are the most good looking guy I ever met and you're just amazing and you're so different from anyone else and you're my little pet… you're so special… *(Pause. They all stare at him) I am!* I… I… I… I… I… I… am! *Toby! Toby!* The woman conceived and bore a son; and when she saw that Toby was a fine Toby, she hid Toby three months. When she could hide Toby no longer she got a papyrus basket for Toby, and plastered it with bitumen and pitch; she put the Toby in it and placed it among the reeds on the bank of the river. Toby's sister stood at a distance, to see what would happen to Toby. The daughter of Pharaoh came down to bathe at the river, while her attendants walked beside the river…

ANN. Please!

THOMAS. *(Enters)* Stop it now, Toby!

(Thomas pulls out a gun and points it at Toby. Toby stops for a minute. Silence)

CHARLIE. Oh, Thomas, put the gun down!

THOMAS. Shut up!

TOBY. *(Slowly)* Are you going to shoot me?

THOMAS. If you don't stop talking nonsense, yes I will!

TOBY. *(Pause. Takes a deep breath in)* Thomas, in the beginning when Toby created the heavens and the earth… *(Small pause, then he starts talking faster. All the other characters talk whilst Toby is talking)* … The earth was a formless void and darkness covered the face of the deep, while a wind from Toby swept over the face of the waters. Then Toby said, "Let there be light"; and there was light. And Toby saw that the light was good; and Toby separated the light from the darkness. Toby called the light Day, and the darkness he called Night. And there was evening and there was morning…

THOMAS. Toby, I'm not joking! Shut up… You have ten seconds!

ANN. Thomas! Toby, please! Let's go away from here! Charlie, stop him!

THOMAS. Ten… Nine…

CHARLIE. Tom, Let him go!

THOMAS. No! He can't go! He just can't! Eight… Seven… Six… Five…

ANN. Toby! Please! Thomas! No!

THOMAS. Four... Three... I'm going to do it! I'm going to shoot!

CHARLIE. Don't worry! He's not gonna shoot him!

THOMAS. Two... One... BANG!

TOBY. ...the first day...

(Toby falls on the floor. They all stand quietly. Ann is the first to move. She goes to Toby and starts sobbing. Charlie follows her)

CHARLIE. *(Very cold)* You killed him! What did you do that for? Tom... You can't just... You can't!

THOMAS. No! *He* couldn't! He's mine!

ANN. Oh my God!

CHARLIE. What?

ANN. *(Touches his wound and looks at her hand)* Those are tears...

BERNIE. *(Enters wearing a party hat. No one moves. She doesn't notice Toby, and she walks around and puts party hats on Thomas, Charlie and Ann)* Happy New Year, my dear... May there be no tear or fear or whatever the hell it was! I forget that bloody rhyme… where's Toby? He'll remember. Oh, I'm so sorry I missed the countdown, I could hear it from outside. *(Yells offstage)* Toby… I want to kiss you! *(To the others)* Why are you all so quiet? This party is so dead! Are there many people here? Oh well… Have no fear, Bernie is here! I brought this brilliant cassette with loads of oldie songs on it… it's hilarious! It's just so funny! You've got to put it on *(Bernie takes the cassette out and gives it to Thomas. He ignores her)* OK… so I'll put it on, shall I? *(Bernie puts it on. The song "Jack in the box" by Clodagh Rodgers plays… She starts dancing)*

Happy New Year!

ALL. *(Each in his own time)* Happy New Year!

$ellebrity

$ellebrity was first performed at The Blue Elephant Theatre, London, between 11-29 of May 2010 as part of Naughty! with the following cast:

The Girl	Kate Chisholm
The Star	Ido Gonen
The Friend	Jo Saddler-Lovett

Lights come up on a man sitting tied to a chair
The Girl is sitting opposite him and smoking a cigarette
He is gagged
There is a long silence

THE GIRL. I love you so much. No, seriously. I know everybody tells you that, but I really do. You are amazing.

Stop

I voted for you every week, like a gazillion times.

Stop

You don't know this, but we actually know each other. My sister's boyfriend's neighbour is Dr Pelcher, your dentist. And then in week four, you had that tooth-ache, and I knew it was a sign.

Stop

Don't look at me like that. I'm not crazy. I'm not like your other fans that are obsessed with you and all that – I don't even like your singing voice that much. But you've got a heart of gold. You should've won that show. You are such a beautiful person, and like… you know.

Long Stop

Do you want a fag?

Stop

I remember seeing you in the first audition, and you seemed so shy and… what's that word… Come on… fuck! It's in the bible. Jesus like says it or something. What is it?

Long Stop

Meek! That's it. You were like so meek. And your mother had just died. That was like so sad. I was really upset. But then you sang to her and I like cried. And I know the judges cried too, but I don't think everybody noticed that. I mean, your mother had just died. And you had the courage to come and sing for her. That is like so amazing. I didn't think they'd let you through to the next level, but they like so did. It was so brilliant. And that's when I knew. That's when I knew that you are special. Honestly, this has never happened to me with anyone out of any of these shows. I'm telling you. I'm not some celebrity freak that just chases all these stars and is totally obsessed with them. I don't even like Brad Pitt. But you're special.

Long Stop

Thank you for coming over. I'm really glad you came. You know, I've been dreaming about what I am going to say to you when you finally come over. And I had all these conversations in my head, and it was all prepared and planned, but I forgot all of them. I can't remember. I don't even remember what I wanted to cook to impress you, I can't remember how to cook.

She laughs for a while, realising he isn't laughing with her, she stops

I'll order pizza.

Stop

You know, I changed my dentist. I started going to Dr Pelcher. I thought that maybe I'll see you there. Well, when I saw in week four that you had a toothache, I knew it was a sign, so I started going to Dr Pelcher.

Stop

He's a shit dentist. And anyway, you weren't even there. I paid so much money for a stupid filling. He's an idiot. But I knew there was a chance that we could meet. Imagine that. I sit in the waiting room, my mouth is in agony. I scream, I cry. I'm like so distressed, and from the other room I can hear the drill and some fat old woman screaming and I'm terrified. You see, I hate dentists. Really hate them. So anyway, you come in and you see me. A damsel in distress. And you look at me and it breaks your heart. So you come and sit next to me. Then you take my hand and you look straight into my eyes and you smile, and I already start calming down. So there's a moment of silence and we stare into each other's eyes and for a brief second the whole world like disappears and it is so calm and peaceful, but then the drill starts again in the other room and that fat old woman starts crying again and I get like so distressed again so you start singing. You start singing the most beautiful song and I melt. And everything is all right. And even my toothache goes away and you just pick me up and you carry me out to the car park and we start like kissing and stuff and then ...

Stop

Well. It doesn't matter.

Long Stop

Can I kiss you?

Stop

No, you're right. I shouldn't. That will give you the wrong impression. I'm not that easy. You need to sing for me first. Will you sing for me?

Stop

OK. I'm going to take the gag off you. And you will sing for me, right?

Stop

OK.

She takes the gag off
Stop

THE STAR. Can I have some water, please?

THE GIRL. Oh, shit. You've been thirsty all this time. I am so selfish. I'm really sorry. I was talking and talking and talking about all these stupid dreams and all that and you're sitting here dying of thirst. I didn't mean to do that. I don't want to kill you or anything. You know? I'm sorry.

Stop

I'll get you some water.

She goes out for a moment
The Star tries to wriggle out of the chair but fails
She returns with a glass of water

THE GIRL. There you go.

She gives him the glass and realises his hands are tied
She pours the drink into his mouth and he drinks it in one go

Wow. You were thirsty.

THE STAR. Thank you.

Long Stop

What do you want from me?

THE GIRL. Want?

THE STAR. Yes. Why am I here? What do you want from me?

THE GIRL. You're here because you want to be here.

Stop

Don't you?

THE STAR. I…

THE GIRL. Do you remember week seven? When you were like really ill and you started coughing in the middle of the song and that stupid ugly judge was telling you that you're not professional? I voted for you from like nine of my mobile phones, just to make sure you got through. I was so pissed off. I even sent a letter to the judge. He never got back to me.

Stop

I didn't send you any letters, though. I thought that you should be left alone. You had so much crap to think about and you really needed to concentrate on the show so you could win.

Long Stop
She lights a cigarette

I was gutted, you know? I was really heartbroken when you lost. You should have won, you know.

Stop

You know what I loved most about you? When you lost, you didn't pretend that it was alright. You had that one beautiful tear coming down the corner of your eye. I could see how upset you were. You looked amazing. All I wanted to do was to come over and give you the biggest hug in the world and tell you that you are a superstar. And you were so much better than that blonde girl. She was crap. I can't believe she won in the end. I bet in two years' time we won't even remember who she is. Do you want a fag?

THE STAR. I don't smoke.

THE GIRL. Of course not. That would ruin your voice. I read that in your autobiography. Does it bother you that I'm smoking in here?

THE STAR. No.

THE GIRL. Good. I don't think I could stop, even if you asked me to. I feel like there's so much I want to ask you. I'm just a bit… I'm a bit nervous. Can you tell?

THE STAR. Not really. You seem pretty calm.

THE GIRL. Yeah, well I'm not really. I'm like so nervous. I've been dreaming about this moment for ages but didn't really think it would happen. Are you hungry?

Stop

THE STAR. You know, people are going to wonder where I am. They're going to start looking for me.

THE GIRL. So?

THE STAR. So they might think you kidnapped me or something like that.

THE GIRL. Don't be stupid. How on earth are they going to find you here? Nobody knows you're here. Nobody saw me or you or anything. I wouldn't worry if I were you. You're being a bit paranoid.

THE STAR. How long will you keep me tied to the chair? I'm due at a shop opening tomorrow.

THE GIRL. Not long.

Stop

He looks at her, confused

THE STAR. Are you going to release me soon?

THE GIRL. Of course.

Stop

THE STAR. And then I could go home?

THE GIRL. Of course. What do you think I am? A psycho?

Stop

THE STAR. So… I'm confused. Why am I tied to a chair?

THE GIRL. Just for the time being.

THE STAR. What do you want from me?

THE GIRL. Want?

THE STAR. Look. I'm really confused. Why am I tied to a chair?

THE GIRL. Uhm… I really don't want you to run away. Not yet.

THE STAR. Yet?! I don't understand this yet. What am I waiting for? What are you waiting for?

Stop
The Girl turns shy all of a sudden

THE GIRL. My friend is coming over. She wants to meet you.

THE STAR. Your friend?

THE GIRL. Yes.

THE STAR. To meet me?

THE GIRL. Yes.

THE STAR. And then you will let me go?

THE GIRL. Of course. She has to be home by six.

THE STAR. OK. When is she coming?

THE GIRL. She's on her way. She should be here any minute.

THE STAR. Don't you want to untie me?

THE GIRL. I can't.

THE STAR. Why not?

THE GIRL. Well, she paid for you to be tied up.

THE STAR. Paid for me to be tied up?

THE GIRL. Yeah.

THE STAR. I don't understand. She's paying you to meet me.

THE GIRL. Yeah.

THE STAR. But why does she want me to be tied up?

THE GIRL. I don't know.

THE STAR. How much are you charging her?

THE GIRL. It's none of your business.

THE STAR. Of course it's my business. You're selling me and you're not telling me how much for? Don't I get a cut?

THE GIRL. A cut?

THE STAR. I don't understand why you should get all the money for this. If she's paying money to meet me – I should get some of the money. If you want a commission, that's ok. Like an agent or something. But I should get the lion share.

Long stop
The Girl stares at him and then starts laughing

THE GIRL. No! Do you know how much money I spent every week voting for you? Do you realise how much I had to put into it? The amount of hours I spent in front of the telly watching you and those other idiots sing. I could've spent that time on more productive things.

THE STAR. That is ridiculous. You are being completely stupid. How dare you?

THE GIRL. How dare I?!

THE STAR. Yes. This is not the way things work in the real world. Perhaps in your little tiny insignificant life, that's how things are done, but in the real world I should get at least 50 percent of the money.

THE GIRL. I don't remember getting 50 percent of your money.

THE STAR. I don't remember you doing anything to deserve it.

THE GIRL. I voted for you!

Long stop
They stare intently into each other's eyes, each challenging the other
As the tension rises, there's a knock on the door
The Girl breaks her gaze joyfully

THE GIRL. It's her.

The Girl goes to open the door and comes back with The Friend

THE FRIEND. Oh my God. Oh my God. Oh my God. Oh my God. Oh my God. Oh my God. Oh my God. Oh my God. Oh my God. Oh my God. This is like unbelievable. I can't believe it. This is like. I mean. I just can't believe it. I won't believe it. Can I touch him?

The Girl nods
The Friend touches The Star's arm

Oh my god. This is like so amazing. I mean. It's actually him. It's actually you. I have watched you every week. I never voted for you. I voted for the cripple but you were amazing. Well, not vocally. You were just all right vocally, but you were so funny. Like in week two when you poured the glass of wine over the judge. That was hilarious. Best TV moment in like ages. So, yeah. It's you. I mean, it's actually you.

Stop

She comes close to him

Listen.

Stop

Thank you.

Stop

No, I really mean it. Thank you. You have given me hours of entertainment and I don't feel people like me thank people like you enough. I think you deserve more appreciation so seriously – thank you.

As she continues talking, she starts undressing

So like I am so excited that you're here. I mean, I can't believe that this is actually happening. And can I tell you something? You are so much better-looking in reality. I mean reality reality. Not reality as in reality TV. I mean the real reality – the proper one. Do you know what I'm talking about? The one that's like where we are like conscious and… no. Wait. We are like conscious in reality as well. Wait a minute. Sorry. I am so nervous. I always talk rubbish when I'm nervous. Am I talking too much? Am I scaring you off? I hope I'm not scaring you off. I'm going to touch you again. On your cheek. Is that all right? I just want to feel your skin. Oh wow. It's like so smooth. Thank you. No, seriously. Thank you. You're like so amazing. I mean. Not vocally. But who cares about vocals? Talent isn't just about vocals. Not that you have real talent.

She looks at The Girl

Oh, God. I mean, I didn't mean that you're not talented. I don't mean to offend you. I just meant that you can't sing...

She is about to take her shirt off when The Star interrupts her

THE STAR. What are you doing?

THE FRIEND. Uhm... taking my shirt off!

THE STAR. Why?

THE FRIEND. I've had lots of fibre today, and my five-a-day and I'm ready. Would you prefer I do it with my shirt on?

THE STAR. Do what?

Long stop
The Friend looks at The Girl and then back at The Star again

THE FRIEND. Sex. Didn't she tell you?

THE STAR. No. She didn't tell me.

THE GIRL. You don't need to know everything. It's not like you have to prepare for it. Like one of your songs.

THE FRIEND. Not that he ever prepared.

THE GIRL. Hey, Shut up.

THE STAR. Yeah. Shut up.

THE GIRL. Hey, don't be rude to her!

THE STAR. We are not going to have sex.

THE FRIEND. Do you just want to give me your sperm, then?

THE STAR. My sperm?

THE FRIEND. Didn't they teach you in star-school about the birds and the bees? Yeah. I need it in order to get pregnant by you. I am ovulating today. It's perfect.

THE STAR. Pregnant?

THE FRIEND. Yeah. I paid good money to have your baby.

Long stop

THE STAR. You want to have sex with me in order to have my baby? Alright, but why do you want to have my baby?

THE FRIEND. Are you kidding me? You are so good looking and so sweet.

THE GIRL. You are, you know.

THE STAR. Of course I know.

THE FRIEND. I want my baby to be just like you.

THE GIRL. Hey, your baby might be a pop star, too.

THE FRIEND. Oh my God. I didn't think about that. How amazing would that be?

THE GIRL. I know. And then he could like sing for you.

THE FRIEND. Well, if he gets his voice from me. Oh, and just like his mother, I could die just before he goes to audition and write in my will that I want him to still go, and then he'll dedicate every song to me.

THE GIRL. Wow. You'll be like a dead popstar's mum... No, wait. That doesn't sound right.

THE FRIEND. No, I'll be dead. Not him.

THE GIRL. Yes… You'll be a dead mother's popstar.

THE FRIEND. No, that still doesn't sound right

THE GIRL. A mother's dead popstar?

THE FRIEND. Hmmm…

THE GIRL. You'll be a dead celebrity. And everyone will see your photo all the time.

THE FRIEND. Can you imagine?

THE GIRL. That's like so amazing.

THE STAR. My mother was shot to death. That is not genetic – especially not to you!

THE FRIEND. Whatever. Then his stardom will pay my mortgage.

THE STAR. I can't understand how you would consider selling my sperm to someone without giving me any of the profit.

THE FRIEND. You're not sharing the money with him?

THE GIRL. You know how much money I've spent on voting for him?

THE FRIEND. Oh, yeah. That's true. She did.

Stop

All right. Let's get it over and done with.

She hitches up her skirt and sits on The Star's lap
The Girl opens a bag of crips and starts eating it whilst watching

THE STAR. Look. I am really not comfortable.

THE FRIEND. Oh, sorry. Would you rather do it on a bed?

THE STAR. I would rather not do it at all.

Stop

THE FRIEND. But… I've paid a lot of money.

THE GIRL. She did. She paid a lot of money.

Stop

THE STAR. Really? How much money is a lot of money?

THE GIRL. I'm sure it's nothing compared to the millions you're making now, but it's enough to cover my costs for voting for you.

Stop

OK. Hurry up. You need to finish with him quickly so that he can regain his energy and do me.

THE STAR. Look, this is really inappropriate. I don't think there is any justification for this kind of behaviour. I demand to get some humanitarian rights. This is simply unjust.

THE GIRL. Do you want me to I don't gag him?

THE FRIEND. Oh please. Would you?

The Girl gags The Star

THE FRIEND. That is so much better. Like, seriously, I don't like your voice. Right. Let's do it.

The Friend pulls up her skirt, opens The Star's fly and sits on him

THE FRIEND. Yes! He's wearing boxers.

THE GIRL. How is it?

THE FRIEND. Flaccid. Come on. Pump some blood into it. Do you need me to kiss you or something? Hurry up. I don't have too much time. I have to be home by six.

THE GIRL. Maybe it's because you offended his singing.

THE FRIEND. Do you reckon? Is that it? Is your ego damaged?

He nods shyly

Oh… I'm like so sorry. Look, it's just a matter of taste. But you are so hot. And your voice is good. Isn't it?

THE GIRL. Yeah. I love it.

THE FRIEND. Tell you what. Would you like to sing something now, while we do it?

He nods

All right then.

She takes his gag off
He starts singing Somewhere Over The Rainbow
The Friend begins to move on top of him in rhythm
The Friend takes her mobile phone out of her bra and takes a photo
As the song climaxes, so do they
The Friend gets up as The Girl claps and cheers
The Friend lays on her back with her legs in the air and bounces a few times before getting up and getting dressed

THE GIRL. That was beautiful.

THE FRIEND. It wasn't too bad.

THE GIRL. No, I like seriously have a tear in my eye. That was like so amazing

THE STAR. Really? Do you really think so?

THE GIRL. Oh, wow. Yeah. Of course. Can I have a go?

THE STAR. Sure.

THE FRIEND. Right, I'd better go and take some folic acid. I've not exercised in weeks to make sure it happens. All right. Thank you. This was lovely. Best I ever had. Well, thanks for that. Good luck with your career.

The Friend leaves
Long silence

THE GIRL. So…

THE STAR. So…

THE GIRL. How was it?

THE STAR. It was all right.

THE GIRL. Just all right?

THE STAR. I would have enjoyed it more knowing that I get some of the money.

THE GIRL. You know, I've got some more friends that would totally want to get pregnant by you.

THE STAR. Really?

THE GIRL. Oh yeah.

THE STAR. Will I get a cut?

THE GIRL. Sure.

THE STAR. How much?

THE GIRL. I'll give you ten percent.

THE STAR. That sounds fair.

THE GIRL. I can let you go now.

THE STAR. I thought you also wanted to do me.

THE GIRL. You don't have to be tied for that.

THE STAR. No, I guess I don't.

She unties him as the lights go down
Blackout